The Bill of Materials in Excel, ERP, Planning and PLM/BMMS Software

Shaun Snapp

The Bill of Materials in Excel, ERP, Planning and PLM/BMMS Software

Copyright © 2013 by SCM Focus Press

For information about this title or to order other books and/or electronic media, contact the publisher:
SCM Focus Press
PO Box 29502 #9059
Las Vegas, NV 89126-9502
http://www.scmfocus.com/scmfocuspress
(408) 657-0249

ISBN: 978-0-9837155-2-8

Printed in the United States of America

Cover and Interior design by: 1106 Design

Contents

CHAPTER 1

Introduction

Background and Motivation

This book is an attempt to educate readers about the enormous inherent limitations and inefficiencies of the current software approaches being used to manage the bill of material (BOM). My view of the state of BOM management results from years of working on projects

1

and from seeing companies repeatedly make the same mistakes, costing them in multiple ways.

Companies may be affected adversely by the common approaches to BOM management in ways such as those listed below:

1. Longer product development lead times

2. Lower quality final product

3. Higher management and coordination costs

4. Maintainability issues

5. Less efficient internal manufacturing planning

6. Reduced ability to leverage or maintain contract manufacturing relationships

The above issues can be greatly mitigated by following the approaches to designing the bill of material management solution laid out in this book. Those who specialize in BOM management system implementation have known these approaches for some time; however, for whatever reason the information has not caught on with the vast majority of companies.

Step 1: Understanding the Design Conceptually

The first step toward understanding the design that I propose in this book is to understand how various software applications interact with and manage the BOM; a difficult topic if a comprehensive approach is not taken. Similar to the story of the four blind men who derived their disparate descriptions of an entire elephant by touching isolated parts of the elephant's body, it is not sufficient to study the BOM from the perspective of one system only.

"In various versions of the tale, a group of blind men (or men in the dark) touch an elephant to learn what it is like. Each one feels a different part, but only one part, such as the side or the tusk. They then compare notes and learn that they are in complete disagreement.

The stories differ primarily in how the elephant's body parts are described, how violent the conflict becomes and how (or if) the conflict among the men and their perspectives is resolved."

Therefore, this book takes a comprehensive perspective regarding the BOM.

Step 2: Understanding the BOM in Various Software Applications

Once the interaction between various software applications and the BOM are understood, the next step is to learn how to leverage applications that use the bill of material. I believe that individuals have difficulty understanding the BOM in its comprehensive form because existing literature does not include application screenshots to show how the BOM looks in different applications. While some product manuals produced by the BOM management vendors come close and are quite good, the manuals focus exclusively on a particular vendor's application and do not show how the BOM looks in competing applications. As a result, few people get the benefit of a comprehensive education in this area, one reason as to why BOM is so poorly managed in general.

This book is such an opportunity for readers to understand the BOM in various software applications as it pulls together material that previously has been available only in isolated sources and presents the information in a complete form. While this book is limited to a single master data object (the BOM), it follows the BOM through several applications, making the book broad in its coverage. At the same time, this book provides a high level of detail and connectedness, while keeping the topic understandable.

The book provides a foundation of understanding and also recommendations that naturally follow from an enhanced comprehension of the bill of materials. None of the recommended approaches are particularly expensive, and in fact, this book is more about the application of knowledge in the key leverage points rather than wholesale changes or major redesigns.

My Background

I work across multiple supply chain software areas in my consulting practice, and the companion website, SCM Focus, covers a wide variety of supply chain software. I have written books on SAP APO (advanced planning software), supply planning software and demand planning software. For the reasons expressed previously in this chapter, I was motivated to write a book on the bill of materials. However, I have one other reason. From my experience, improving the approach to BOM management can result in one of the highest returns on investment of all enterprise software applications. I have witnessed many BOM management implementations (as outlined in these pages), and there is a significant difference between how I see BOM managed in spreadsheets and ERP systems versus BOM management suites. I have tested the systems that enable BOM management and have compared the results to those my clients obtain using their systems and the discrepancy is always great. In fact, one of my regrets is that I am normally dedicated to working on the supply chain planning application and I am not able to address or get mindshare on the opportunity for better BOM management. This means that I often sit by while very poorly constructed BOM management strategies are followed. I have concluded that, for the most part, the very interesting story and benefits of modern BOM management is not getting out. The mistakes you will see me describe in this book are not simply the observations of a few projects, but of every project I have worked on. I am amazed as anyone that BOMs are still managed so poorly, but there is no way of getting around this fact.

I am a supporter of many best-of-breed supply chain planning applications and I write about them quite extensively. However, if I were heading up a major implementation and had to choose between supply chain planning applications and BOM, I would probably elect to perform the BOM management implementation first for the following reasons:

1. The inherent improvements resulting from a true BOM management solution are so great.

2. Many other supply chain applications themselves rely upon the data provided by the BOM.[1] As I will show, they represent a subset of the data that is kept in the BOM management system.

---

[1] I am not the only person to make this observation. Antti Saaksvori and Anselmi Immonen state "... PLM can result in impressive cost savings, with many companies reporting pay-off periods of one to two years or less based solely on reduced product development costs."

3. BOM management systems tend to be far less expensive and have higher implementation success ratios than supply chain planning applications. The current cost of the Arena Solutions product is approximately eighty dollars per person (i.e., seat) per month. I point this out to undermine the argument that these solutions are expensive.

For me, the decision to first upgrade the Bill of Material Management System, or BMMS, is an easy one.

Currently the two most common approaches to managing BOMs are:

1. To manage them directly in the ERP systems

2. To maintain them in spreadsheets and then manually upload them to the ERP system

As I will demonstrate, efficiently "managing" a BOM in an ERP system is impossible because ERP systems lack the full complement of fields that make up a BOM. Second, managing a BOM in a spreadsheet is problematic because spreadsheets are essentially sophisticated flat files. While Excel has a number of advanced features for data management, which I frequently use myself, spreadsheets are best for representing information that is not nested and not related to many other categories of data. Flat files and spreadsheets can easily represent hierarchies with codes; for example, they can be used to maintain forecasting attribute files, which are then loaded into the forecasting application (I describe this process in detail in my book *Supply Chain Forecasting Software*). However, applications specifically designed for the task — and not spreadsheets — are best used to manage hierarchies and relationships. Further on in this book I will explain how the best BOM management software adds significant value to the BOM by creating a high degree of relatedness with a wide variety of BOM information.

The Software Discussed in This Book

The ERP software showcased in this book is SAP ERP, or SAP R/3-ECC, and I've done so for two reasons. First, I am familiar with this software and I have access to it. It also happens to be the best selling ERP software in the world, and so many readers will see an application that they use in their workplace.

At times it may seem that I am critical of SAP's BOM management functionality in this book; however, while I don't step away from this criticism, similar criticism applies to other ERP vendors as well. This criticism is necessary because the BOM management is often presented incorrectly to executives as something that can be performed effectively and efficiently by the ERP system. While never actually true, this misinformation is less true now more than ever as BOM management systems have rapidly developed over the past several decades. Although both of the largest ERP vendors, SAP and Oracle, have product lifecycle management (PLM) offerings, the fact is that ERP vendors in general have been presenting an over-simplified fiction of BOM management to executive decision makers. Most of these executive decision makers have never personally worked in a role where they managed a BOM. Because of exceptionally misleading information by vendors who need to protect their ERP applications for becoming exposed regarding how they mismanage BOM data, I have attempted in this book to unravel misimpressions that have been created over many years by many vendors. Major ERP vendors, while having very little knowledge for how to properly manage BOMs, nevertheless have a very powerful influence on how they are managed. How little do the large ERP vendors know about BOM management? That is easy to determine. Simply walk onto any major ERP implementation; if no BMMS solution is in place, you will find major BOM management inefficiencies. Other non-ERP applications that rely on the BOM tend to not understand BOM management very well either. These vendors want to make a sale, and one of the best ways to do this is to talk about how integrated they are with ERP systems. If you check many non-ERP vendors websites, you will find them littered with various certified (by the ERP vendor) integration adapters. (Most of these certified adapters are more marketing sizzle than reality as the link below describes.)

http://www.scmfocus.com/sapintegration/2011/11/15/what-are-saps-vendor-integration-certifications-worth-on-projects/

For non-monopoly vendors, it is crucial to show the ability to integrate with one of the monopoly ERP vendors. Therefore, they often pay homage to the existing ERP system during the pre-sales presentation at the client by stating that they will simply extract the BOM from the ERP system, which they state is the system of record for the BOM. Of course in the vast majority of cases, this is true, the ERP system is the system of record of the BOM, but as you will see in this book, it should not be. Therefore, ERP systems have inherited the role of BOM management, even though they are not up to the task.

Other Books on the Bill of Material

In most cases, the literature review required when preparing to write a book is a good deal of work. Books are only one part of the review (although outside of promotional literature and software vendor manuals, there is not a great deal written on the bill of materials). The literature review for this book did not take very long because there are only a few books written specifically on the BOM, although many books cover the BOM in a chapter or as part of a chapter. The major works on the BOM are *Bills of Material: For a Lean Enterprise,* and *Manufacturing Data Structures: Building Foundations for Excellence with Bills of Materials and Process Information.* The BOM is addressed in a number of other books, including a book by one of my favorite authors, George Plossl, *Structuring the Bill of Material for MRP.*

While the BOM is a very important topic, it is a topic which is both under researched and under published, and much of the information about BOM management is quite dated. For example, even though the copyright date of one of the books is 2010, in fact the vast majority of the book was written in the mid-1990s. George Plossl's work goes back to the 1970s and 1980s and *Manufacturing Data Structures* goes back to 1992. What this means is that all of the books on the BOM predate the development of BOM management systems! For instance, I am confident that George Plossl would have covered the BOM differently if he had exposure to a modern BMMS. In fact as I will show, some of the decisions that are presented in these books as necessary, turn out to be unnecessary when modern BOM management software is used. The good news is that many rules of thumb that required structuring the BOM in a way that limited its flexibility is no longer necessary. With the right software and the right approach, BOM management can become a major source of competitive advantage for a company rather than a headache and limiting factor for other applications that rely upon the BOM.

PLM Versus the BOM in Popular Literature

Given the limited published information available on the BOM, one initially wonders where decision makers are getting their information about how to intelligently manage the BOM. In order to find out, one must expand the literature review beyond BOM to include PLM (Product Lifecycle Management), because for some time (and even up to the present day) BMMSs were sometimes referred to as product lifecycle management or PLM systems. This nomenclature was actually an unfortunate but conscious linguistic obfuscation made by the management at some software vendor and then copied by other vendors, eventually becoming standard terminology in the field. This decision never made any sense logically, but at any time there are illogical and terminologically incorrect marketing initiatives at many enterprise software vendors. In the enterprise software space, product sales success trumps all normal accuracy standards. This is why it is quite dangerous for company executives to read vendor literature without having it screened by content experts in the literature's field that are paid by the implementing company, but also do not receive a financial benefit (i.e. a consulting company) from uncritically analyzing information provided by the software vendor.

The decision to standardize around the term has actually resulted in slowed development in this software area. Because the term PLM is so poorly defined, vendors who don't really have a solution have been able to pose as if they do, resulting in a great deal of confusion for clients. What has become evident is that many highly-paid marketing professionals at software vendors have been unconcerned with even elementary accuracy, that is accuracy in terminology.

Further on in the book I will discuss in detail a BMMS vendor named Arena Solutions, a thought leader in this software segment. They have correctly moved away from branding their BMMS applications as a PLM application.[2] However across the software segment, it is a mixed bag with regard to terminology,

---

[2] I have witnessed this several times in my analysis of various best-of-breed vendors like Arena Solutions, where the software vendor with the best offering is also the thought leader. Other examples include MCA Solutions (since purchased by Servigistics) in service parts planning, and Demand Works for supply chain forecasting. (Both of these vendors are showcased in my other books, which were influenced by their user manuals.) What "thought leader" means is that the vendor produces some of the very best written material on the topic, including all Internet sources, books, academic papers, etc. The material can take the form of blog posts or software manuals, as software vendors rarely write books. One of the best ways to understand an application area is to identify the software vendor thought leader and gain access to their user manual. I have learned an enormous amount by following this approach. However, the strategy does not generalize; most vendors do not emphasize excellence in writing, and their software manuals and related materials sometimes provide little insight beyond why you should buy their applications or simply how to operate them.

as Siemens and Agile still use the term PLM to describe their applications. Unfortunately, using the term PLM to describe a single application simply makes no sense because lifecycle planning is comprised of a large swath of functionality, which is distributed throughout a wide variety of enterprise applications. For instance, lifecycle functionality exists in product design systems, demand planning, supply planning and also production planning, as well as ERP and the BMMS. Demand planning applications typically have a segment of their functionality dedicated to lifecycle management, however, the BOM for the most part is never part of demand planning applications. Nevertheless, PLM applications do overlap with BOM management solutions, meaning it is necessary to evaluate the books on PLM as well, including *Product Lifecycle Management* by Michael Grieves, and *Product Lifecycle Management: 21st Century Paradigm for Product Realization* by John Stark. These two books approach BOM management from the management perspective. The only book on PLM that has any real overlap with software concepts is *Product Lifecycle Management* by Antti Saaksvori and Anselmi Immonen. This book explains the BOM from the strategic perspective and how to think of and implement PLM/BOM systems into the enterprise. I found myself conflicted when reading this book because in some paragraphs the authors describe PLM as an umbrella term, which I think is the correct interpretation of the term PLM, but in other cases when the term PLM is used, the authors actually mean the BOM management system. Again, BOM and PLM are not the same thing.

The authors of these books evidently understand the importance of software-enabled BOM management and make the case—the same case that I make in this book—that BOM/PLM is a tremendous opportunity. All of my previous books have focused on supply chain software. I wanted to develop a book that described the following vision through text and supporting screenshots: integrating applications with the BOM management solution as the central hub and which feeds other systems that rely upon BOM information. A central premise of this book (and one that it is very straightforward in making) is that attempting to manage the BOM without a BMMS does not make a lot of sense. This book will outline how a BMMS is used, and how it integrates with all other systems that use bill of material information.

Many authors are reticent to say anything particularly controversial or to say things they know to be true, and many don't want to deal with controversy. However, many true observations never get printed without accepting some conflict. As a reader of many supply chain and IT books, I am sometimes frustrated that after investing the money and effort in buying and reading a book, I often come away feeling that the author has not been completely forthright. I tend to gravitate toward authors who are willing to put themselves on the line to tell the straight story. Anyone who has read http://www.scmfocus.com, knows that the site does not shy away from controversy. This book takes the road less travelled and points out things that have worked and things that have not worked, both of which are equally important. In addition, it diverges from the antiseptic approach taken by many books on the topic.

The Importance of Software Screenshots and Vendor Diversity

Unlike most books about software, this book showcases more than one vendor. Focusing an entire book on a single software application is beneficial for those that want to use that application. However, only the biggest vendors such Oracle and SAP tend to get books that showcase their applications. This necessarily leaves out a lot of other vendors with quite educational and interesting functionality. I prefer to include examples of software from multiple vendors. However, it's also important for the reader to understand that I am completely independent from all the software companies. The specific application screenshots used in this book were selected because I found them to be good examples of functionality in an area, and they helped me demonstrate a concept.

I consult in some popular and well-known applications, and I've found that companies have often been given the wrong impression of an application's capabilities. As part of my consulting work, I am required to present the results of testing and research about various applications. The research may show that a well-known application is not able to perform some functionality well enough to be used by a company, and point to a lesser-known application where this functionality is easily performed. Because I am routinely in this situation, I am asked to provide evidence of the testing results within applications, and screenshots provide this necessary evidence. Furthermore, some time ago it became a habit for me to include extensive screenshots in most of my project documentation. A screenshot does not, of course, guarantee that a particular functionality works, but it is the best that can be done in a document format. Everything in this book exists in one application or another, and nothing described in the book is hypothetical.

How Writing Bias Is Controlled at SCM Focus and SCM Focus Press

Bias is a serious problem in the enterprise software field. Large vendors receive uncritical coverage of their products, and large consulting companies recommend the large vendors with the resources to hire and pay consultants rather than the vendors with the best software for the client's needs. Just as in my consulting practice, I do not financially benefit from a company's decision to buy an application that I showcase in a book. SCM Focus has the most stringent rules of any information provider in the space with regard to controlling bias and restricting commercial influence. These "writing rules" are expressed in the link below: http://www.scmfocus.com/writing-rules/

If other information providers in this space followed these rules, I would be able to learn about software without being required to perform my own research and testing projects on every topic.

Information about enterprise supply chain planning software can be found on the Internet, but it is primarily promotional or written at such a high level that none of the important details or limitations of the application are exposed; this is true of books as well. When only one enterprise software application is covered in a book, the application works perfectly; the application operates as expected and there are no problems during the implementation. This is all quite amazing and very different from my experience of implementing enterprise software. However, it is very difficult to make a living by providing objective information about enterprise supply chain software, especially as it means being critical occasionally. I once remarked to a friend that SCM Focus had very little competition in providing unvarnished information on this software category, and he said, "Of course, there is no money in it."

Making the Perfect Book for Those Hungry for Precise Information on the Bill of Material

By writing this book, I wanted to help people get exactly the information they need without having to read a lengthy volume. The approach to this book is essentially the same used in my previous books.

1. **Be direct and concise.** There is very little theory in this book and I do not spend any time covering much more than simple math.

2. **Clearly define the different categories of software that use BOM information.** Simply understanding how various software uses BOM information can place a company on the right course when designing their supply planning solution.

3. **Based on project experience.** Nothing in the book is hypothetical. I do not include concepts or applications that cannot do exactly what I say they can. I am not here to "sell" software to anyone, but to use software to demonstrate how to improve BOM management. Many of my experiences are based in seeing the BOM being managed incorrectly, even when very expensive supply chain planning and ERP applications are connected to it.

4. **Saturate the book with graphics.** Roughly two-thirds of a human's sensory input is visual, and books that do not use graphics—especially educational and training books such as this one—can fall short of their purpose. Graphics have also been used consistently and extensively on the SCM Focus website. Before writing this book, I spent some time reviewing what has already been published on the subject.

The SCM Focus Site

I am also the managing editor of the SCM Focus site (http://www.scmfocus.com), and, therefore, the site and book share a number of concepts and graphics. Furthermore, the book contains many links to articles on the site, which provide more detail on specific subjects. This book provides an explanation of how a variety of supply chain software works—BOM management as well as production planning and supply planning. The SCM site dedicated specifically to supply planning is http://www.scmfocus.com/billofmaterials/.

Use of Quotations

This book makes frequent use of quotations, which were recorded during the research phase of the book writing process when I found many insightful comments from several sources. Some of my favorite quotations came from the documents produced by Arena Solutions, and these quotes were very effective at providing additional information about aspects with which I did not have direct project experience.

A guide for authors that I had previously read stated that one should limit the usage of quotations and try to rephrase the author's comments into one's own writing whenever possible. I believe they teach this approach in some college writing courses. I have to say I completely disagree with this sentiment. An effective document in a technical field triangulates with the other existing material. This is not to say that one must agree with the quotation and in fact I list several quotations, which I think are out of date given recent software developments. (This should not be seen as criticism of the authors. The authors were writing before some of the software described in this book existed.) I simply do not feel that paraphrasing quotations is the correct way to go about writing the book. I have always been in favor of using quotations and I use them liberally on the SCM Focus website. In fact, I frequently add a quotation after a post is already published because I find a new spin or unique insight on the topic from an author. I also recall teaching supply chain for a year, and how I was irked at reading student papers that did not include a quotation where one should have been included; that is, some sentences came across as minor rewrites of what was obviously someone else's idea. I also have a problem with white papers placed on the web as promotional literature by software or consulting companies that not only lack quotations, but footnotes as well. Some of the best-known consulting companies leave footnotes out of their white papers. This creates the illusion of innovation where none exists. I was once told by Andersen Consulting to not mention that found an innovative way to handle inventory management problem from a book by George Plossl. Andersen Consulting wanted to leave the impression that I had come up with the idea on my own.

BOM Terminology

(Throughout this book I will use the term BOM for convenience, economy of expression and consistency. However, if the reader works in a process industry the term formula or recipe may be interchanged every time I use the acronym BOM.)

My Relationship with Arena Solutions

While I am an advocate for Arena Solutions, it will be of interest to readers that I have no financial relationship with them. I am not placed on projects or recommended for projects by them and in no other way benefit from any improved visibility they may receive from either this book or several articles I have written about them at SCM Focus. They have a partnership program, but I do not participate in this program except to occasionally view the recorded webinars. Unlike large consulting companies or analyst firms, SCM Focus has a nonfinancial relationship with all of the vendors we write about and the other software vendors I showcase in this book. My income is derived from working as an independent consultant directly to companies on implementations, diagnostics and solution evaluations on SAP projects, and a much smaller amount from books. Interestingly, I have received several emails over the years that essentially state if SCM Focus is as independent we say I say it is then why do I write positive reviews of some applications. In a way I don't understand the criticism because independence means that one is not influenced/compensated, etc by the entity they are describing. Being independent does not mean that one does not have opinions. For instance, a movie reviewer who is independent of studios will still find movies that they rate highly and movies that they do not. The problem with our present enterprise software evaluation system, be it the analysis provided by consulting companies or software analysis, is not that they are overly opinionated about software they esteem or do not esteem, it is that they have financial ties to the vendors they evaluate. On the other hand, I have been also criticized for being critical of products that I work with. I was once told by a consultant in an email who worked in the same product that I did that he did not think it was right for me to publicly write articles critical of the same application that I made money in. My response to him that in that case he was opposed to objectivity as a general principle.

Some of these types of comments have lead me to conclude that the term "biased" is used quite flexibly by some segment of the population, and that they use the term to mean with "disagree with me." That is if you agree with them, you are unbiased, if you disagree with them, then you have a bias. What is quite amazing is that the major consulting companies, that only recommend software of vendors that they have relationships with and can maximize their revenue from recommending, are very rarely described as having a bias. Secondly, this is not some incidental behavior of these companies, but the heart of the business model of the major consulting companies. This is clearly an example of slavishness to large institutions. If a company is large, it is naturally deferred to regardless of their financial benefit from recommending partner vendors, while SCM Focus, being small, is much more likely to be criticized for bias, even though there is absolutely no income received through recommending one vendor over another.

Who Is This Book For?

The feedback I received from early reviewers is that this book is an effective primer for anyone who:

- Is looking to perform a BOM management software selection

- Is beginning a BOM management project at their company

- Wants to see the most advanced approach to managing the BOM

If you have any questions or comments on the book please email me at shaunsnapp@scmfocus.com.

Abbreviations

A listing of all abbreviations is included at the end of this book.

CHAPTER 2

An Introduction to The Bill of Materials

For many people who purchase this book, a BOM may seem like a well-defined and relatively straightforward master data object. Because this book will approach the BOM from a broader perspective than the reader may be used to, this chapter lays down the foundation of many of the topics I will describe in this book. Let's start off with what Wikipedia has to say about the BOM.

A list of raw materials, sub-assemblies, intermediate assemblies, sub-components, components, parts and quantities needed to manufacture an end product.

A BOM can define products as the following:

- *As they are designed (engineering bill of materials)*

- *As they are ordered (sales bill of materials)*

- *As they are built (manufacturing bill of materials),*

- *or as they are maintained (service bill of materials)*

In the process industries the BOM is also known as the formula, recipe or ingredient list.

The first hierarchical databases were developed for automating bills of materials for manufacturing organizations in the early 1960s.

A bill of materials implosion links component pieces to a major assembly, while a bill of materials "explosion" breaks apart each assembly or sub-assembly into its component parts.

— Wikipedia

For a conceptual explanation of what an effective BOM management system can enable, I quote from Antti Saaksvori and Anselmi Immonen:

> *The core of product lifecycle management is the creation, preservation and storage of information relating to the company's products and activities, in order to ensure the fast, easy and trouble-free finding, refining, distribution and reutilization of the data required for daily operations. In other words, work that was once done should remain exploitable.*

Important BOM Features

The three most important things to understand about a BOM are as follows:

1. The BOM contains information about how to design and build a product.

2. A BOM is a master data object. This means that it is one of the elements that sets the boundary for the model that is the enterprise application.

3. A BOM is a hierarchical or nested structure containing product information.

I found it interesting that the BOM was the original reason for the development, at least partially, of the hierarchical database. Hierarchical databases were the first to be developed and, except for some very specialized purposes, have been completely replaced by relational models. Of course, relational databases can represent hierarchies without any issue, and all software that I am aware of presently that has a BOM, represents it in its data layer using a relational database. However, the fact that BOMs were a major impetus for the development of the first computerized database design indicates how elemental they are to business. The following image shows the multi-level nature of the BOM.

Multi-level BOM Example

This screenshot of a multi-level BOM shows the Printed Circuit Board Assembly (PCBA) in a GPS product.

The following quote, which describes multi-level BOMs, is from *Managing Multi-Level BOMs,* by Arena Solutions:

> *A multi-level BOM, also referred to as an indented BOM, depicts parent-child relationships and shows the hierarchical structure of assemblies and their related parts and components. A multi-level BOM is essentially a nested list whose parts or items are listed in two or more levels of detail to illustrate multiple assemblies within a product's BOM. In contrast, a single-level BOM depicts one level of children in an assembly and only the components needed to make the assembly are listed.*

BOMs in Many Places

As has already been discussed, one of the confusing features of a BOM is that it exists, albeit in different forms, in many different systems, meaning that what a BOM looks like to a design engineer is quite a bit different than how it looks to a supply chain planner, including how large and detailed the BOM is and how frequently it changes. For instance, a BOM in a BMMS is highly detailed and changes frequently. On the other hand, a BOM in a planning system is typically updated periodically, or when a new product is introduced or is removed from the database. There is a positive relationship between the detail in the BOM and its volatility or how much it changes. The BMMS is designed to manage this volatility in a way that no other application does.

When a master data object is shared among multiple applications, it is important to declare which system is the system of record. The system of record is the authoritative source of information. When a system is identified as the system of record for a master data object, this means that (ideally) all changes should be made in the system of record and then fed to the "child" systems. The system of record can be a table or a spreadsheet. Whichever system of record is used, it should be capable of managing the master data object for which it is assigned. It also must be comprehensive, meaning that the system of record must store the full complement of fields that make up the master data object. The problem with BOM management historically is that systems chosen as the system of record for the BOM have met neither of these criteria. Historically, spreadsheets have been the most common system of record, although many companies do not have one system of record for the BOM. Instead, different groups that are responsible for the operation of various systems maintain different information about the BOM in different systems, resulting in data inconsistencies, visibility issues and archival issues. The BOM is then disjointed and its ability to be managed and leveraged for future products is compromised. Some people think that the ERP system is the system of record, but as I will show in several ERP screenshots, this is not really possible.

This is a material in SAP, which is then part of a BOM or multiple BOMs. However, it is important not to confuse this representation of materials and BOMs that are in all ERP systems with a BOM management solution.

However, one problem with attempting to make the ERP system the system of record for the BOM is that not everyone uses the ERP system. This problem is described below by Arena Solutions:

> *Engineering groups are often not inclined to use ERP systems unless absolutely necessary. While a manufacturing BOM and associated item data are usually loaded into an ERP system to manage production sourcing and costs, ERP systems are not designed to be change control or file management tools. Consequently, all changes to items and BOMs have to be recorded, approved and tracked outside the ERP system. Additionally, ERP systems are primarily used by limited groups within a company and generally are not accessed by outsourced partners or suppliers. They do not provide project collaboration capabilities that are necessary to successfully manage product development tasks and milestones across a global supply chain.*
>
> — "Beyond BOM 101: Next Generation Bills of Material Management,"
> Arena Solutions, 2011

Making design engineers use the ERP system to access the BOM has been attempted many times and is a losing strategy. Enterprise software implementation is interesting in that it is almost never analyzed historically in order to determine what has worked and what has not worked. Or is it: Therefore, large numbers of clients continue to use failed strategies regardless of the outcomes. ERP systems are only set up for internal access by the company's own employees. Except for the SaaS ERP systems, which are a very small proportion of the overall ERP market, most ERP systems do not have HTML interfaces and cannot be accessed by supply chain partners. Secondly, the representation of the BOM in both ERP systems and external supply chain planning systems is so simplified that compared to the original BMMS BOM, it is a "baby BOM."

When there is no single system that manages the overall BOM, different groups maintain different parts of the BOM separately in different applications, resulting in the different BOM types.

The Different Types of BOMs

The major BOM types are as follows:

1. The Design or Engineering BOM

2. The Manufacturing BOM

Other important BOM types are:

1. Costing BOMs

2. Plant Maintenance BOMs (not relevant for producing items)

3. Sales BOMs (defines the product as it is ordered)

The manufacturing BOM (MBOM) resides in the BMMS (if one has been implemented), ERP system or— if the company uses an external production planning system, —then in both the ERP system and in the production planning system. External planning systems are normally fed by the ERP system, so the BOM in the each system is essentially the same.

The design or engineering BOM (EBOM) is maintained in the design systems and, of course, in the BMMS. Both the supply chain systems and the design/ engineering BOMs can only represent the MBOM and EBOM respectively. However, the BMMS can represent the MBOM and the EBOM, as well as additional information not contained in either BOM. This is why the BMMS must be the BOM system of record. Additionally, the BMMS is the BOM archival system and should contain BOMs going back many years as well as the intermediate states and previous versions of BOMs. Holding this BOM history is extremely helpful for engineering and design as they can look through old BOMs to determine whether to bring back a previous BOM or to create a new BOM by copying an old BOM and revising it. In addition to the product-specific data, the BMMS also holds the supplier relationships, along with suppliers who were included in the initial request for proposal but were not ultimately selected. This allows the design department to leverage all the previous work when creating a new product. While supply chain systems have no need to maintain this information, by having the supplier or contract manufacturer information, design and engineering as well as contract negotiation can send out the design specifications for subsequent

RFPs to companies that were not selected previously for a particular BOM but may be selected in the future.

As the system of record for the BOM, and by supporting design and engineering, the BMMS will contain many more versions of the BOM than will reside in supply and production planning systems or the ERP system. Supply chain planning and execution systems only require the BOM versions that are currently in production and that are slated to be produced in the future. These applications manage the life cycling of BOMs with something called "effectively dates." However, BOMs that are no longer being used can be purged from these systems. A positive aspect of implementing a BMMS is that it takes the load off of BOM archival in other systems. In fact, the BMMS' ability to improve the management of the BOM in other systems is one of its frequently misunderstood benefits. Many executives only see the BMMS as another set of interfaces they have to write, without considering that the BMMS pays back the effort of interface development by providing far more efficient BOM management that in turn, improves all the applications that rely upon BOM information.

Old BOMs should not be purged from the BMMS system unless they truly represent products that the company no longer makes and they contain no information that can be leveraged for future purposes (i.e., because the records represent the BOM and design history of the company, and because old BOMs can often be adjusted and copied over as future BOMs). Maintaining all previous BOM data in the BMMS increases the value of BOM information within a company: decades of BOMs can be stored, reviewed and altered as future BOMs, all in a way that provides maximum traceability and reusability. Arena Solutions brings up the following point with respect to BOM archival:

> *Most companies like to reuse parts from current products when they develop new products, as a way to both purchase in larger volumes and reduce engineering and manufacturing risks. But when products are designed by different teams, commonalities can be missed.*
> — "Beyond Colored Folders and Spreadsheets: Next-Generation Document Control for the Medical Device Industry," Arena Solutions, 2011

The benefits of this are extremely apparent to anyone who works in this area as is described in the following quote:

> *Over time, Arena becomes the repository for institutional knowledge:*
> *records of how certain design challenges were solved, how iterations*
> *of innovative technology were developed and how the product*
> *development process was handled. Arena captures and securely stores*
> *product data, for reuse and analysis.*
> — "Collaborative Tools for Product Development: A New Approach,"
> Arena Solutions, 2011

By archiving BOMs in the BMMS, the burden is removed from all BMMS satellite systems to maintain BOM information themselves, meaning that the other systems are free to maintain only the current BOMs — a welcome relief to the teams that support the systems. Generally speaking, when a supply or production planning system is used (or an ERP system for that matter), far too much legacy master data objects are left over from previous use, which makes finding the current master data objects cumbersome and time consuming. I once worked for a client that had ported over an installation of SAP APO from their European operations. APO is SAP's advanced planning system. In doing so, they did not purge any of the European data; it was necessary to scroll through all the European locations to bring up the North American locations. A lot of time was being wasted when performing searches for locations and other master data elements in the system. It takes longer to troubleshoot and to perform simple tasks like finding valid product-location combinations with systems that contain large amounts of unused master data. In this case, all of the master data existed in the European installation of the application, so there was no reason to keep this data in the US system for archival purposes. It is more beneficial to remove unused data at the earliest convenience, and to either delete the data or export it to an archival system.

I have seen supply chain planning implementations postponed or halted because the company could not get a handle on their BOM variants (different versions of similar BOMs). Here's an example from one company with which I consulted. During the implementation, the number of BOMs required exploded when the implementation team began to visit factories and found that the small number of BOMs they had planned to model would not represent all of the BOMs in each plant. The number of BOMs increased again when accounting became involved and demanded that many costing BOMs (that is, additional BOMs that are necessary to represent the different costings associated with different manufacturing processes—I discuss this in more detail in Chapter 5: "The Bill of Material in ERP and External Planning Systems") be included in the scope of the project. The problem was that the company was attempting to manage all of these BOMs in a spreadsheet. These many BOMs would have been far easier to manage had the company invested in a BMMS system, a system that would have cost them very little compared to the costs of extending the production planning project deadlines.

Master Data Management and the BOM

A BMMS can be interpreted as any of the following types of systems:

1. A content management system

2. An associative application

3. A product design management system

4. A collaborative system

5. A supplier and contract manufacturer management application

6. An archival system

7. The system of record for BOM data

However, while the BMMS is all of these things, it is also an excellent master data management system, albeit only for the BOM master data object. Many systems make it difficult to maintain and effectively view and control all types of master data (many vendors' systems specifically lack aggregated views or efficient ways to get a comparative understanding of the master data). While this book does not focus on master data management, the following links provide several articles on issues with the present way of managing master data, as well as some alternatives:

http://www.scmfocus.com/supplychainmasterdata/2012/02/an-approach-for-improving-master-data-maintenance-better-than-mdm/

http://www.scmfocus.com/supplychainmasterdata/2011/04/master-data-management-using-excel-and-powerpivot/

In fact, one of the easiest consulting contracts for me involves diagnosing systems with poor master data, because poorly maintained master data is so easy to find, and so many companies are unaware of how out-of-date the master data is in their SAP planning applications. A common mistake is to blame the functionality for the poor master data, when in many cases the master data parameters settings have simply not been maintained properly. One reason it is so easy for me to find poorly maintained master data is because SAP does not do an effective job of exposing the master data to users. The business, which actually has the information to update the master data, is often not prepared to make the changes in SAP, and instead need IT to help make many — if not most — of the master data alterations.

Understanding the Different Dimensions of Master Data Maintenance
One issue with master data is the ease with which it can be updated and another is the ease with which it can be found and viewed, and SAP has many limitations with both issues. Generally speaking, the solutions that have been presented in the Master Data Maintenance (MDM) space are poor. I have never seen a solution with the MDM moniker that actually adds value on a project. In fact, I have referred to MDM projects primarily as boondoggles.

http://www.scmfocus.com/supplychainmasterdata/2010/06/why-software-based-mdm-is-a-consulting-boondoggle/

MDM projects also tend to be too ambitious, trying to do much more than simply serve as an effective repository for master data. The MDM consultants become overly infatuated with words like "taxonomy" and the solutions themselves are too theoretical and not really designed for the most important aspects of managing master data.

I would like to find a SaaS solution for MDM that I could recommend to clients, because this would make the application easier to access and maintain, especially for those clients with global operations. An SaaS solution could allow those that update master data to make their updates from anywhere in the world in the cloud solution, and then the master data could be reviewed at a central location before updating it to SAP. While I have not heard SaaS discussed very frequently in regard to MDM, it is clearly a natural fit. However, up until this point, all MDM solutions have been lacking whether on premises or SaaS. The article at the following link describes my search for an MDM solution that actually makes sense and is compelling for a client.

http://www.scmfocus.com/supplychainmasterdata/2012/06/master-data-management-in-the-cloud/

The best application that I have used for maintaining master data is actually Arena Solution. *However, it is only designed to control BOM information.* My clients need something like Arena Solutions, but for all the master data objects and not only for the BOM. Creating such an application is a difficult task, because the solution provider must know all the fields to be maintained, and must also know their names or be able to map their names to the MDM system. However, the fact that I am searching for master data management solutions and Arena Solutions is the model for what I would like to see, says good things about Arena's ability to serve as a master data system of record for BOM data.

Integrated Solutions

ERP and supply chain planning system really only need materials and BOMs when these systems are ready or planned to be put into production. Eric Larkin of Arena Solutions has the following to say about companies that attempt to manage their BOMs with ERP software. "ERP, planning and design, and engineering solutions need to work in conjunction with BMMS systems to create a collaborative environment, both internal and external to the company, and that provide a high degree of functionality and control over the BOM. The BMMS is constantly being accessed, changed, updated, and leveraged for collaboration."

http://www.scmfocus.com/failedsupplychainconcepts/2010/10/eric-larkin-from-arena-solutions-on-companies-that-attempt-to-manage-their-boms-with-erp-software/

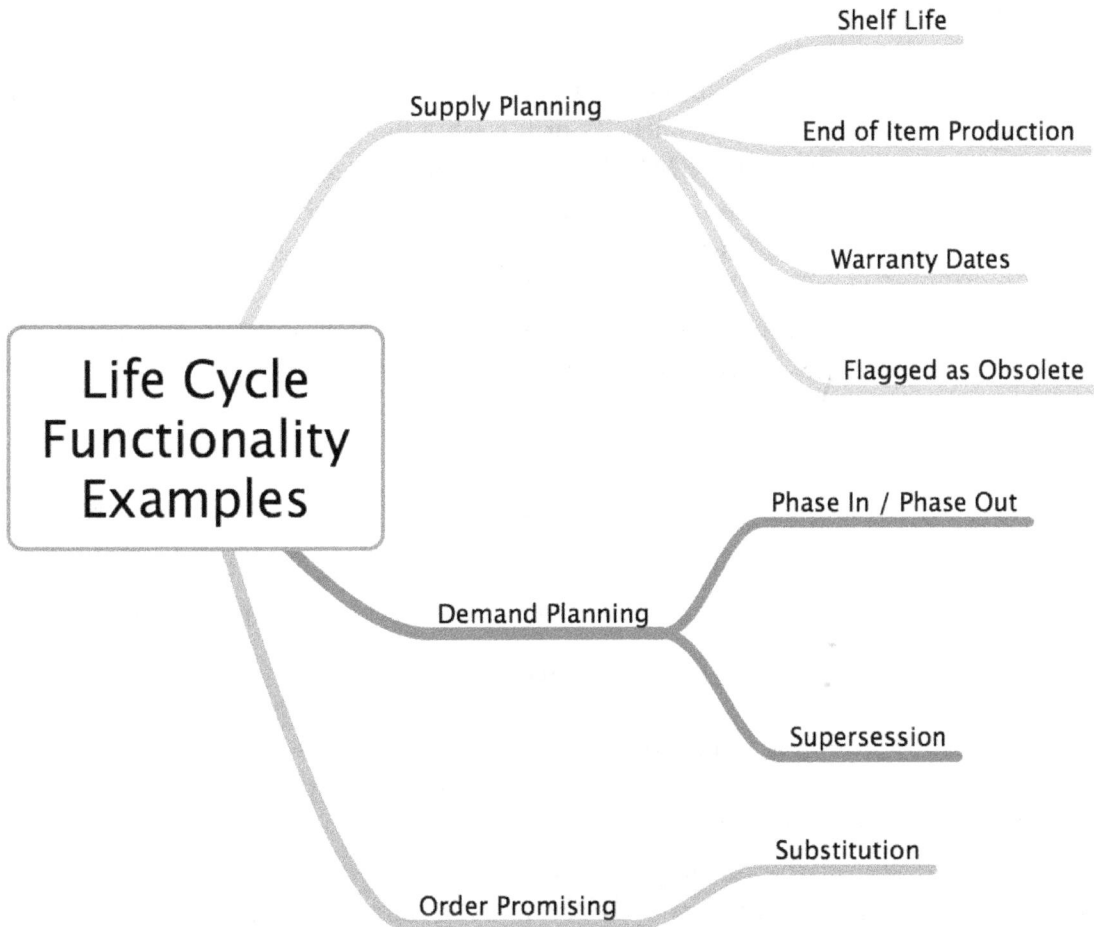

Supply Planning
- Shelf Life
- End of Item Production
- Warranty Dates
- Flagged as Obsolete

Life Cycle Functionality Examples

Demand Planning
- Phase In / Phase Out
- Supersession

Order Promising
- Substitution

None of these discrete areas of functionality have anything to do with turning over BOM records; in fact, they reside in planning systems that are not the system of record for BOMs, but instead only copy the material and BOM records from the ERP system on a periodic basis. Secondly, this is not a complete list as there are lifecycle areas of functionality within ERP that are also unrelated to BOM management. I simply listed the areas of lifecycle functionality with which I have firsthand experience.

Conclusion

Traditionally, a BOM is simply considered to be a master data object, more limited than what I describe in this book. Whether you agree with the limited definition of a more expanded view may change based upon which software is being discussed. For example, in applications with a limited representation of the BOM, the traditional definition is correct. However, the broader definition is more applicable to advanced applications that specialize in BOM management. As such, BMMS software has essentially enlarged what is represented by a BOM. In fact, a major strength of a BMMS is that it integrated the master data object with the other data associated with the BOM, making the BMMS a very powerful application for understanding, storage and collaboration on the BOM. BOMs can be differentiated into EBOMs and MBOMs, and in fact, the only real term that is not helpful in describing the BOM is "product lifecycle management" (PLM), which is something I explained in Chapter 1: "Introduction."

Three of the most important features of a BOM are the following:

1. The BOM contains information about how to design and build a product.

2. A BOM is a master data object, meaning that it is one of the elements that sets the boundary for the model that is the enterprise application.

3. A BOM is a hierarchical or nested structure containing product information.

The fact that BOMs look very different depending upon which system they are implemented in creates a problem in understanding the BOMs. This, along with confusing terminology (i.e., PLM) and misinformation on the part of ERP vendors, has greatly hindered the development of a full understanding of the enterprise BOM. Another factor hampering BOM management is that the applications that companies choose to be the system of record for the BOM typically cannot represent the BOM in a complete manner and/or are not effective systems for the task, even for the most elementary requirements of a BOM system of record. When the BOM is distributed among various systems, with no single system of record for all BOM information, the company's capabilities with respect to product data—from every dimension—greatly decline, and the company can be said to be "BOM inefficient." Most companies do not have a single system of record for the

BOM, leading to all types of knowledge gaps between a company's departments. When a company cannot effectively associate data that interacts with the BOM within a single system, and does not have a system that can be effectively shared and used for collaboration with suppliers and contract manufacturers, the result is internal and external gaps in BOM management.

A big benefit of a BMMS is its ability to reuse BOM data and is, in fact, a very strong argument for its implementation. First, new products are based upon old products, and in many cases are highly derivative of old products. While the vendor might tell their customers that there are big leaps between old and new products, the company's engineers know that this is not the case. Second, while companies push the idea that they are constantly innovating, the marketing department knows that derivative products are far more likely to succeed than entirely new products. In fact, one of the major assets of manufacturing companies is their storehouse of information about products that have worked in the past. They also know which suppliers to rely upon for which parts, and they know the costing of each of the parts, as well as the price points of previous similar products so that they can more easily estimate the profitability and therefore the desirability of a new product. This is a company asset, which can be further enhanced with a BMMS. Arena highlights this point with the quotation below that describes BMMS systems, which are SaaS based:

> *BOM (and associated item specifications, sourcing, and pricing data) has traditionally been viewed as the final deliverable from the design team to manufacturing, but the BOM is very well suited to capturing and organizing product data throughout the design as well.*

> *Both technical and non-technical users are generally familiar with the BOM as a conceptual model and are able to easily navigate the BOM to find relevant product cost data. In addition, IT support because the data is stored in a secure database outside the company firewall and accessed using web browsers, IT support is not needed to install client software or to allow design or supply chain users to view the data. Finally, the problem of controlling supplier access to product cost data can be handled with component sourcing relationships that*

> *automatically define "need to know" relationships between supplier*
> *users and product data: suppliers can see product data for only those*
> *BOM items for which they are identified as a source.*
> — "Manufacturing Outsourcing: Seven Common Pitfalls to Avoid," Bijan
> Dastmalchi, Richard Vermeij, Arena Solutions, 2007

The easiest and most efficient way to develop a new product is to copy over an old product BOM, and then make changes to the parts of the product BOM (which may be a very small subset of the overall BOM) that will make the product considered a "new" product. This BOM copy can be performed quickly in a BMMS, and all of the associated data is copied as well, including the suppliers for each BOM, costing, etc. Maximum reuse allows a company to introduce new products at minimal effort. Companies can choose to use the BMMS in a basic way, or to deeply analyze the BMMS for historical information. Arena Solutions sees their software as having the potential to be used in the following way.

> *Over time, Arena becomes the repository for institutional knowledge:*
> *records of how certain design challenges were solved, how iterations*
> *of innovative technology were developed and how the product develop-*
> *ment process was handled.*
>
> — Arena Solutions

The potential to do all of this is there, but of course the company must be sufficiently sophisticated. Simply put, the implementation of any BMMS system will not guarantee that that benefits described above will be accomplished.

This leads to the topic of archival. Archival is of course necessary for reuse and is an automatic feature of a good BMMS. Other systems that rely upon the BOM and use BOM information generally should have their BOM information purged, because maintaining large numbers of BOMs in systems other than the BMMS does not make sense. Keeping the BMMS as the system of record reduces the complexity of these systems and makes them easier to maintain, at least with respect to the BOM. This leads to the topic of the BMMS as the master data management system for all BOM information.

Master data is a constant problem at companies. One issue is that many vendors do not make their master data easy to find and easy to change. I, along with many other people, wonder why vendors can't simply allow spreadsheet uploads to their systems. I describe in the following article how being able to load an enterprise application from a spreadsheet can be beneficial:

http://www.scmfocus.com/supplychainmasterdata/2011/04/master-data-management-using-excel-and-powerpivot/

Second, software vendors have received little payoff after investing heavily in Master Data Management (MDM) applications. In an MDM application, master data changes are centralized and standardized within the one application, rather than dealing with master data in different and less efficient ways in separate applications or sets of applications installed from one vendor. We do not have effective MDM solutions, even though there is a great need for them. Instead of effective or good MDM solutions, we have a lot of talk about "data governance" and lots of glossy product brochures from various software vendors. Most MDM solutions have been designed to be installed on a company's premises rather than to be used via SaaS. However, master data changes are highly distributed inside—and increasingly outside—the company[3], making a SaaS-based MDM highly preferable to an on-premises MDM application. Up to this point, the pickings are slim here as well, a topic which I describe in this article:

http://www.scmfocus.com/supplychainmasterdata/2012/06/master-data-management-in-the-cloud/

In addition to everything else a BMMS does, it is also an MDM solution, albeit only for BOM information. A BMMS meets all the criteria of being a modern

---

[3] Just because a change is made in an MDM system does not mean it automatically flows through to the production systems. There is a review and approval process.

MDM solution (collaborative, highly secure, archival capability, etc.). In fact, Arena Solutions has the best MDM solution that I have yet seen. Unfortunately, it is an MDM solution that is, of course, restricted to the BOM, and the clients I work with need a comprehensive BOM solution. I have been looking for something like the Arena Solutions solution, but which could carry much more of a company's master data. However, the fact that Arena Solutions has set the bar for master data management in their application is a testament to a job well done.

Effective management of a BOM means allowing the BOM data to work with a variety of systems. A company's BOM database is constantly being accessed, changed, updated and leveraged for collaboration. However, it's not necessary for many of the systems that rely upon BOM information to see all of these changes. Centralizing the changes in a BMMS and having all changes originate from a single system can keep all of the systems that rely upon BOM information in synch. Most of these changes are unrelated to the lifecycle that the BOM is in, but are simply changes that are necessary to keep the BOM up-to-date.

CHAPTER 3

Understanding the Flaws in the Current Standard BOM Solution Design

How a BOM is managed depends greatly upon the level of technology and the effectiveness of the solution employed. This is true of any technology-enabled process, and there is an underlying assumption that companies are using reasonably effective and modern methods for enabling a process. Research into multiple technology areas in supply chain management—in addition to areas such as medicine—indicate that this assumption is incorrect. Companies can and do languish for decades using dated techniques. As I described in detail in my book, *Supply Chain Forecasting Software,* many companies continue to use dated forecasting software that prevents them from doing the most elementary modern forecasting functions. I do these things easily with inexpensive forecasting software, but billion dollar companies cannot do them because they botched their software selection. Software selections, no matter how poorly performed, tend to be solidified in companies for years as those who supported the initial solutions continue to support the solutions regardless of how many problems they cause and how little value they add to business operations. In companies, careers matter more than the value-add of decisions.

Of the different software categories I cover, BOM management is one area where only a small number of companies have made a move to implement a BMMS. For years, a number of BOM management techniques have been recommended, and while these recommendations may have been right for a more basic level of software sophistication, they turn out to be quite counter-productive when a quality BMMS is available. This is why it is so important to re-evaluate the BOM management process when moving toward a more advanced application. Effort is required to understand the differences between poor BOM management and BMMS applications, and it is also necessary to work through a lot of literature on this topic from software vendors that seems deliberately designed to confuse executive decision makers.

However, the changes that can be accomplished by adopting the BOM management solution presented in this book will result in less work and higher quality results than those achieved in BOM management without a BMMS. In fact, simply not having to move through the steps necessary when there is no BMMS is sufficient motivation to obtain a BMMS. To compare BOM management with and without a BMMS and describe the advantages of a BMMS, I present quotes from a popular book on the BOM called *Bills of Material for a Lean Enterprise*. As I stated in "Chapter 1: Introduction," this should not be seen as criticism of this author. This author wrote this before some of the software described in this book existed. However, it is important for those that need to make decisions on the BOM make those decisions based upon the current state of technology.

These quotes present challenges experienced in BOM management in an environment where we can assume a BMMS is not being used. In my responses to each quote, I show how each challenge would be handled by a BMMS.

Statement: *Easier said that done. Blue Bird offered some 900 basic body plans, with many additional options for each body plan, pushing the number of unique buses into the stratosphere. Each bus consisted of between 1800 to 3000 parts.*

My Response: This gets into the topic of configuration, but a BMMS can represent all of this complexity without the need to simplify the complexity for the system.

Statement: One of the tools we use in restructuring a bill is the phantom, also known as a pseudo or blow-through. The phantom is a grouping of parts that may or may not be able to be assembled, used strictly as a convenience in planning and scheduling. Phantoms have numerous uses, but one of their main uses is in helping to cope with products that are offered with many customer specified options.

My Response: The concept of a phantom BOM applies to a dated method of BOM management. Under the old concept, part of the product BOMs is "real," in that the product will be produced. The other part of the product database are "phantom" BOMs. The concept of a phantom BOM loses much of its historical meaning once a BMMS is implemented because the BMMS is filled with BOMs in many different stages of completeness. When a BOM sits in the BMMS, it does not affect any production system. The BOMs that reside in the BMMS can all be considered virtual until the BOM is sent to an ERP system or planning system. The reason why the term "phantom" was used previously is because there was no BMMS in place and it became necessary to draw this distinction. However, with a BMMS there is little need to continue to use the terminology of a "phantom BOM." Instead, a BOM can be created, can be copied from a previous BOM, and can stay in the BMMS in whatever state, in any revision. When it is sent over to a planning or execution system it becomes active, and eventually the inactive BOM will be purged from the planning or execution system. The question that then arises is how long the BOM should be maintained as an archival object in the BMMS.

Statement: A better way of dealing with options and multiple end items is through modularizing the bill of material. Modularizing the bill means grouping parts in a product by the option they're sensitive to. A 220-volt test instrument, for example, requires a different transformer than a 110 volt unit. The transformer, then, is sensitive to the voltage option. By creating bills for each option, not each end item, we have the advantages of fewer bills of material, less bill of material maintenance, more efficient order entry—and easier forecasting of options. After modularizing the bill, we create a planning bill, which is basically a sorting of the Master Bill of Material for planning and forecasting purposes. The modularized bill does allow for much more efficient order entry. The bill can be configured at customer order entry time in such a way as to create the unique bill of material for each customer order. Some companies use a computerized "configurator" system to help speed up this critical order entry time.

My Response: There is no reason to modularize the BOM when one has a BMMS, because the functionality described by modularization is taken care of as an elementary functionality of a good BMMS. This again gets to the superior organization and display capabilities of these types of systems.

Statement: *Although these sub-assemblies exist for a short time, the stockroom issues components, not the coil and switch subassemblies to make the motors. Usually, there is little reason to recognize these sub-assemblies; doing so would only add an extra level to the bill. There are, however, exceptions. Levels in a bill are like the ripples from a stone thrown in still water. They rapidly spread out through the entire company. Only, unlike the ripples, which are constantly decreasing in size as they move away from the event, the ripples from added levels grow until sometimes they achieve tidal wave proportions. The requests for accounting information in the above example translate into hours—and dollars—lost to paper work and shuffling parts into and out of the warehouse. It also implies having a warehouse in the first place, and the personnel to operate the warehouse.*

My Response: The "ripples" listed above are not a problem in a BMMS. However, the quotation does not state where the subassemblies are to be maintained, so one can, of course, choose not to represent them in the ERP or planning system, but have them in the BMMS. The quotation above describes the MBOM, which as has been described, is always a subset of the BOM that is held in the BMMS and contains much less complexity.

Effective BOM Solution Design

The most effective BOM solution design is listed graphically below:

BOM Solution Design

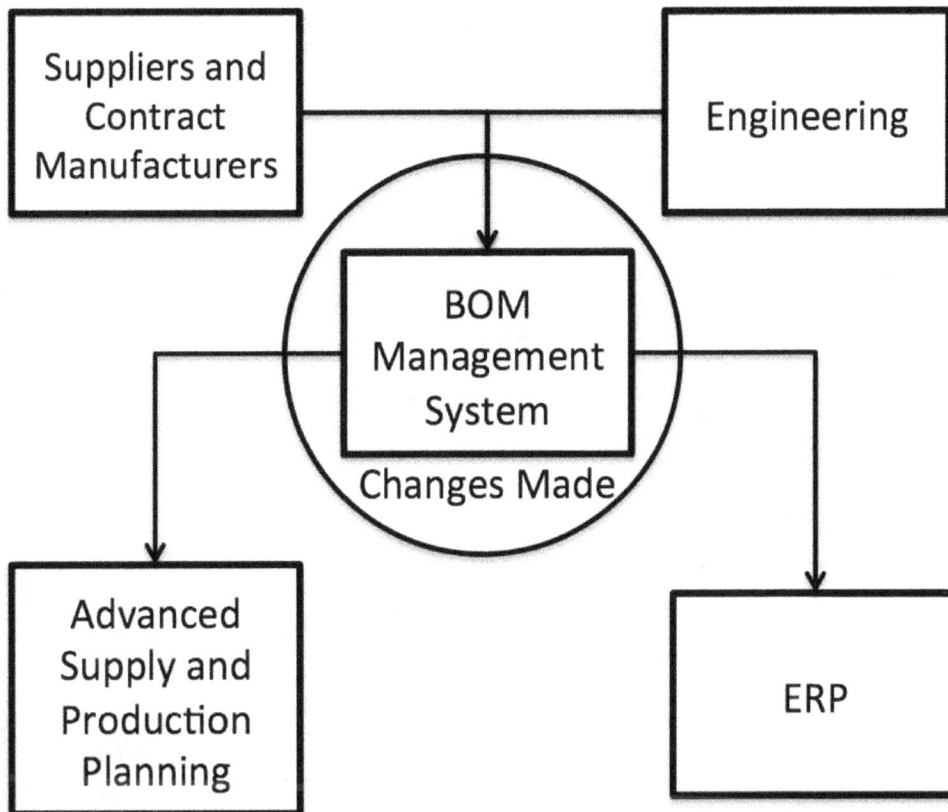

This is a simplified example, and there are more complex designs with many more inter-actions between the BOM and different groups. However, the basic concept is that the changes to the BOM are managed in one specialized application designed specifically for that purpose, (this is the BOM Management Solution or BMMS) and all other systems that require BOM information are satellites of the BMMS.

BOM Solution Design

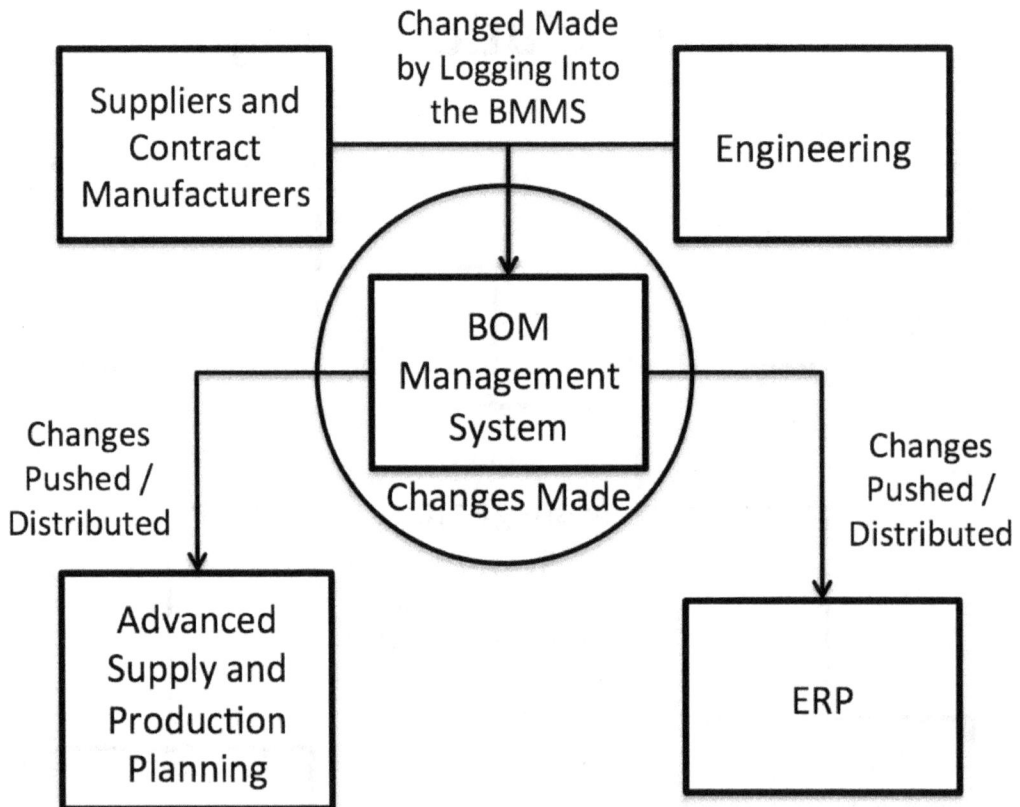

This graphic highlights the fact that different satellites, while all connecting to the BMMS, have different relationships to it in terms of interaction. Both supply and production planning systems and the ERP system are populated with data from the BMMS on a routinized schedule, or even perhaps on a real-time basis. However, engineering, suppliers and contract manufacturers may actually log in to the BMMS itself to review and interact with the system.

This design means that both supply and production planning systems and ERP systems require a data interface to the BMMS (which may, in fact, may only connect physically between the BMMS and the ERP system), with the ERP system relaying the BMMS data to the supply and production planning system through the standard supply and production planning and ERP system interface. Engineering, suppliers and contract manufacturers may not require a data interface, as they would simply use the system directly through the user interface.

What should be immediately apparent is that this sample design is an extremely good fit for a SaaS BMMS. As Arena Solutions describes, the BMMS SaaS solution sits in a protected environment, but outside of the company firewall, allowing both internal and external groups to interact with the application. In fact, at this date, I would question how competitive a non-SaaS BMMS could be with a SaaS design, because of all the limitations of a non-Saas environment. The benefits of a SaaS-based BMMS solution are listed below:

1. The BMMS, being highly accessible, is updated frequently. This means that everyone is working from the same updated copy of each BOM, and they do not fall out of synch with one another.

2. The BMMS has multiple ways of interoperating with different systems and groups. Some groups interact with the system through the interface; others simply need data extracts from the BMMS. (Some companies have BOM maintenance performed in both the ERP system as well as the BMMS; however, this is not a recommended solution.)

BMMS Data Superset Versus the Satellite Subset
Something that is difficult to represent on a graph but that I want to emphasize is that the BMMS and its satellite applications share different types of data. (Of course, which system is a satellite of which depends upon the context of the discussion. This is a BOM-focused book, so I have the ERP system as a satellite of the BMMS. However, if this were a book on ERP, it would be the other way around.) This is shown at a high level in the graphic on the following page.

BOM Solution Design

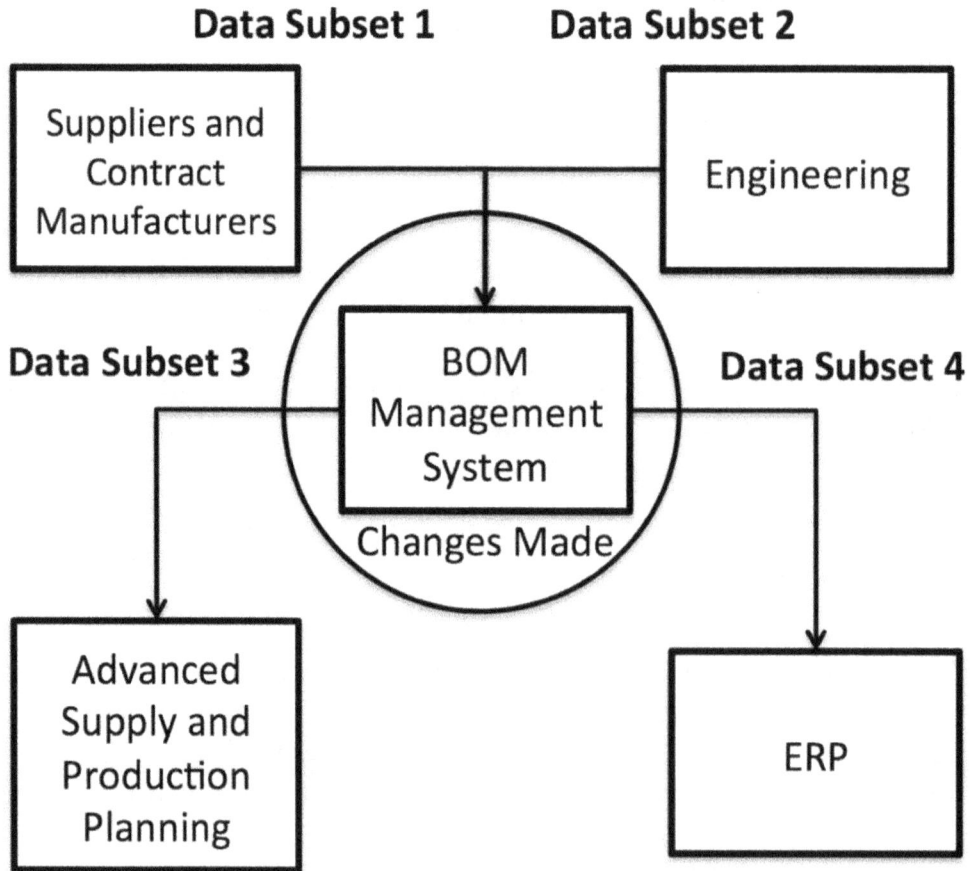

Data Subset 1   **Data Subset 2**

Suppliers and Contract Manufacturers

Engineering

Data Subset 3   BOM Management System   **Data Subset 4**

Changes Made

Advanced Supply and Production Planning

ERP

In this image, I have both supply and production planning systems and ERP systems as using the same data subset—or subgrouping of data—which is a subset of the overall data maintained in the BMMS. However, engineering has a different data subset, which is also different from the subset used by suppliers and contract manufacturers. One perfect example of this is design drawings. Design drawings are part of the BMMS data superset, but are not shared with supply and production planning or ERP systems. Each one of the subsets of data can be called its own BOM, sub-BOM or mini-BOM. However, multiple views on the BOM or BOM types can exist within a BMMS without issue, because data that is stored one way can be displayed many ways depending upon the functionality built into the interface. This resolves one of the major problems faced by companies that lack a BMMS as described in the quote below:

Too many BOMs in too many locations…multiple BOMs floating about on servers, desktops and email, causing confusion as to which one represented the most up to date revision.

Arena provides a single repository for product data and is web-accessible at any time by any authorized employee, partner or supplier.

Redline BOM view in Arena - Compares 2 revisions and displays components that have been added or subtracted, quantities, phases, part names and part numbers which have been modified. Changes in files can also be shown.   4

Notice the revisions above. This shows the user what has been changed, the old number, along with the revised number.

Version control is one of the most important aspects of BOM management. A good BMMS not only keeps all the BOM information in synch, but can also alert people when their BOM has changed.

Through Arena's redline functionality, you cannot miss a change and inadvertently order the wrong part. You can easily compare two revisions of a BOM and see how they differ. — "3 Tips for Effective Product Revision Control and Communication," Arena Solutions, 2011

We have selected the redline functionality but are still on the current working revision. However, if we change the current working revision-to-revision 2, the redline differences can be seen.

It turns out the cap, which was part number 622-9002-1, was replaced with the cap 622-9002-2.

This is described in the quote below:

> *Arena offers layers of protection against ordering the wrong part or making a decision based on out-of-date data. You can impose varying levels of control depending upon where in the process your work is. During early design stages, engineers can control the revisions and can be notified when a new version is available and ready for prototyping.*
>
> — "Three Essential Tips for BOM Control," Arena Solutions, 2011

Change view in Arena - Include internal and external partners in your change notification process, subscribe them to be notified of a change and/or as part of the decision board.

> *Even when an OEM has an internal engineering change order procedure, the CM is often not involved early enough to respond efficiently to the change. For small and medium sized manufacturers, the common method to communicate BOMs and changes is still manual, utilizing phone, fax or email. The fact that these manual ECOs are so arduous often drives people to cut corners in documentation, communication, or gathering input to evaluate the impact of the change.*
>
> — "Collaborative Tools for Product Development: A New Approach,"
> Arena Solutions, 2011

Because Excel does not highlight changes, this leaves users vulnerable to missed changes when reconciling newly-updated BOMs with the master.

This is of course incredibly important. It's much easier to review changes that are made apparent to the user than asking them to catch what has changed by looking through a list. Many engineering and design projects have run into snafus because someone missed an important revision when they were scanning many line items looking for what had changed. With this capability, users don't miss changes and get the wrong part as a result. BOM revisions can also be compared.

Conclusion

The level of technology and the effectiveness of the solution employed have a direct effect on how a BOM is managed. Most companies are managing their BOMs as if we were in a pre-BMMS era, and as a result are imposing a high level of inefficiency on those that work with the BOM both inside and outside of the company. BOM management is one example of a dated approach being applied to problems, but I can easily find examples in other areas that are covered by SCM Focus such as demand planning, supply planning, production planning and detailed scheduling. While some older books present BOM management as requiring a number of important decisions in terms of how the BOM is stored, many of these decisions are no longer necessary with a BMMS. Because a good BMMS can represent the BOM in a variety of ways, the BOM management approach is greatly simplified, and this is an example of how an application can result in a great deal of labor cost savings. Secondly, while these BOM storage decisions in the past limited the ways in which a company could interoperate with the BOM, with a BMMS, the company can gain the flexibility of interoperating with the BOM in a way that meets the need of each group.

The chapter laid out what is, in my view, the most efficient BOM management design. At the center is the BMMS, which serves as the central repository for BOM information and which is the BOM system of record. All changes to the BOM are made in the BMMS, and later copied over to the other systems that use BOM information. The BMMS is where most of the BOM information in the company is stored; all the other systems only have a subset of the BOMs, a subset of the associated BOM information, as well as a subset of the number of versions of each BOM that the BMMS has. During the early stages of each BOM's life, the BMMS is the primary collaboration system for design and engineering with suppliers and contract manufacturers. It also stores detailed costing information for each BOM, and when a new BOM is created, this information can be easily reused and leveraged by copying and renaming a previous BOM. Unlike all other systems that deal with the BOM, the BMMS is effective at controlling and making apparent the changes that have occurred within each BOM.

CHAPTER 4

The Bill of Materials (EBOM) in Design/Engineering Systems

The BOM begins its life in the design and engineering systems as the EBOM. The rest of the company is usually oblivious to—and has little reason to be concerned with—the many BOMs and changes to BOMs made by design and engineering. For the rest of the organization, the BOM only becomes relevant when it is approved to be an actual manufactured or ordered (in the case of contract manufacturing) product. Of course, a great deal of work occurs before this happens:

1. The product must be conceived.

2. It must go through many design revisions and design changes.

3. Suppliers must either bid on many of the input parts (in the case of products that are manufactured internally) or on both the input parts and the overall manufacturing (in the case of contract manufacturing).

The BOM will experience the most active changes during the engineering and design stage. During this stage, design and graphics files are included into the process and added to the BOM. Not all the information that is created in this stage is included in the manufacturing BOM (MBOM). While the BMMS represents multimedia files, the files are initially produced in a separate system, often a Computer Aided Design (CAD) system. Examples of CAD systems include AutoCAD and SolidWorks. These systems may store their data in another system called a product data management (PDM) system. The PDM can be thought of as the central organizing store for the CAD systems. Some companies have the BMMS connected to the PDM.

Sometimes the EBOM is thought of incorrectly as something that merely improves the design and engineering process. While it does this very well, an effective EBOM is also a great benefit to the manufacturing process. As pointed out by an article in Arena Solutions titled, *The Engineering BOM*, an effective EBOM process provides the following benefits:

1. Verification of the first parts coming off of a new tool.

2. Improved purchasing decisions with respect to supply chain management through a combination of improved vendor management and improved information about the vendor(s) that are eventually selected.

3. Improved purchasing pricing by improving the information available during supplier negotiations.

4. A reduction in unnecessary changes in the manufacturing process due to more reliable and detailed information about parts.

5. A reduction in missing parts during the initial production runs on new products.

6. A reduction in the number of incorrect parts procured during initial production runs.

7. A more stable EBOM at the time of hand-off to manufacturing.

8. Higher quality control and more certainty on whether the BOM is actually ready to be handed off to manufacturing. This is an important—and often emphasized—point that is expressed well in a quotation from Arena Solutions:

Engineers are often asked to release designs earlier and earlier even when they are not ready. They must work hard to pass the right and correct information to manufacturing so their design can become a reality. With a complete and accurate engineering bill of materials, the hand-off to manufacturing will be made much smoother.
— "Engineering Bill of Materials: The Ins and Outs," Arena Solutions

In addition to the benefits noted by Arena Solutions, I have observed other benefits, which I have listed below:

1. A quality BMMS reduces the BOM management required for both ERP systems and external planning systems if a BMMS is not in place.

2. A quality BMMS manages BOM information in a far superior way to any ERP or planning system. Essentially, all changes are made in a system with superior BOM management data functionality, and then copied over to the ERP and planning systems.

3. A well-controlled EBOM, and by extension a BMMS, helps prevent errors from reverberating down the line.

In effect, even if the BMMS were not used by design or engineering or by the company's suppliers, by purchasing only one seat of an SaaS BMMS and using it exclusively to serve as the system of record and archival system for its BOMs, a company would significantly improve the condition of any system that relies upon BOM information. Yet so many companies are hard headed and dedicated to managing their BOMs in an antiquated manner, that even this proposal must be "sold" or presented with a guarantee, even when the company essentially incurs either zero or close to zero risk as is the case when an SaaS solution is purchased. The corporate decision-making environment is often illogical. Enterprise application decision-making errors of this type are certainly not limited to BOM management; I have witnessed similar mistakes made in the selection of forecasting applications, as this article describes:

http://www.scmfocus.com/demandplanning/2010/09/why-companies-are-selecting-the-wrong-supply-chain-demand-planning-systems/

The CAD Files Within the BMMS

CAD files cannot be manipulated within the BMMS; rather the BMMS is a repository for the files and allows the files to be exchanged in an organized manner. In many cases, other system users need only to display the graphics files, and so the files may be saved or exported from the CAD system as "view only" files. In other circumstances, the native file format of the CAD system must be saved to the BMMS so that the file may be manipulated in another CAD system, with the revised version uploaded to the BMMS. How often this occurs depends upon whether the company is doing all of its own design work, or allowing design alterations to be made by supply chain partners.

This is a screenshot is from SolidWorks which is a CAD system. Both native CAD files and image exports can be included in the BOM management system.

Conclusion

The CAD system is the point of origin for many of the files created by design and engineering systems. The design and engineering departments make most of the changes that occur to a BOM. A BOM must typically go through many changes, with many revisions being applied to multiple associated files before the BOM is ready for production. The CAD drawings are some of the earliest files that are added to the BOM and are sometimes stored in a specialized CAD file management system called PDM. Either the CAD system is "integrated" to the BMMS or the PDM serves as the intermediary between the CAD system and the BMMS. The PDM serves as the repository of CAD drawings. While some companies have PDMs, many companies do not employ a PDM and instead store CAD files in a normal file folder.

One of the most important things to consider when designing a solution is that the individuals in design and engineering work on systems that are different from the systems used by the rest of the company. Design and engineering use their own systems and their input to the process stops when a product is ready to be manufactured. However, the BMMS can be seen as the system that connects design and engineering and their systems to the rest of the company.

CHAPTER 5

The BOM in Spreadsheets

When spreadsheets first began to be popular, they were adopted rapidly as a tool for BOM management. Spreadsheets are easy to create, and do not require much training to develop. They also provide a great deal of flexibility; fields/columns are easily added and can be color-coded and copied. In the early years of spreadsheets, using them to maintain BOM information was not all bad, considering the alternatives. Keeping a BOM in a spreadsheet is certainly superior to keeping a paper BOM or keeping the BOM in a Word® document.

However, the outcomes and limitations of maintaining BOMs in spreadsheets are known quantities, as there is an extensive history. In fact, the flaw in current approaches to designing effective BOM management solutions is attempting to produce solution based upon tools that are common in any company, but are too rudimentary to offer the correct type of functionality required of a BOM management system. Two important points along this line, which I have highlighted previously in this book, are listed below:

1. Spreadsheets are not competitive storehouses for the BOM or good solutions with which to manipulate the BOM.

2. ERP systems are not good solutions for maintaining the BOM. While it is true that ERP systems must be populated with BOM information in order to work properly, they should never be the primary application for the BOM or be used as the system of record for the BOM.

Unfortunately, the BOM management strategies used at the majority of companies break both of the above rules. Arena Solutions is one of the most vocal companies when it comes to pointing out that spreadsheets are inadequate for the task, as the following quote attests:

> *The modern product record often includes a complex set of hundreds to thousands of structured items. Poring over thousands of rows and columns in a spreadsheet to modify data leads to errors. Because a system of spreadsheets does not have integrated change management capability, changes are difficult to trace...Even after the first product is built, the product record will continue to evolve—due to bug fixes, design improvements, part substitutions or supplier switches—until the product reaches its end of life.*
>
> — "Beyond Colored Folders and Spreadsheets: Next-Generation Document
> Control for the Medical Device Industry," Arena Solutions, 2011

There are major problems with managing BOMs in spreadsheets, as listed below:

1. Hierarchies cannot be represented.

2. There is a lack of authorization control regarding who can make changes to the spreadsheet in its totality.

3. There is a lack of authorization control regarding who can make changes to specific data elements in the spreadsheet.

4. Changes and deletions can be made inadvertently, and these errors can perpetuate as the spreadsheet is shared among various individuals.

5. CAD or multimedia files cannot be integrated.

6. The searching capability is limited.

7. Visibility to either the specific BOMs or to portions of BOMs is difficult to control.

8. There is low collaboration functionality (i.e., the spreadsheet must be sent to other parties).

9. There are issues with version control: which spreadsheet is the most current?

All of these issues are mitigated with a BMMS. With the availability of many better and highly cost-effective options, I am frequently astonished how the old bad ways of BOM management continue to persist. Arena Solutions brings up other issues that make BOM management in spreadsheets difficult, and it's important for any company that continues to manage its BOMs in spreadsheets to know these issues.

- *Modern BOMs are large, complex and ever changing. It is inefficient and error prone to manually make and control changes in their typical spreadsheet format.*

- *BOMs are highly relational and include various associated data and files. Managing across multiple BOMs and their associated data with static spreadsheets is nearly impossible.*

- *ERP systems do not have integral processes for engineering change orders, and cannot be used to control BOM changes or manage associated files.*

- *A modern BOM often includes a complex set of hundreds to thousands of structured items. Even after the first product is built, the BOM will continue to evolve—whether due to potential bug fixes, design improvements, part substitutions or supplier switches—until the product finally reaches its end of life.*
    — "Whose BOM Is It Anyway? A Product Disaster Story: 3 Tips for Taking Control of Your Bill of Materials," Arena Solutions, 2011

Spreadsheet Search Capabilities

Searching can work pretty well on a small spreadsheet with low complexity. However, as the spreadsheet becomes quite large (and BOM spreadsheets must be large unless the company makes only a few products), the ability to effectively search through them is limited. Further limitations in performing effective searches exist if some identical parts have different numbers.

Companies will often use advanced functions in Excel, with the purpose of making the program more capable of managing the BOM. One example is the ability to search for components that are used across products for the purpose of negotiation with suppliers. Finding all of the components is a problem, particularly when an identical component has been assigned different part numbers, meaning that applying a simple filter to the spreadsheet may not work. Advanced functions inside of Excel may be required to enable the planning engineer to perform these types of searches. However, as pointed out by Arena, this solution is filled with problems:

> *Companies often try to solve that problem by adding complexity into their Excel spreadsheet BOMs. They use tactics like item master tabs, lookup formulas, cross-referenced spreadsheets and Visual Basic programming — especially if they have an Excel guru on staff. This works as long as your Excel master keeps the connections up to date so they correctly fill in the cells. But this person is now also a single point of failure in an intricate web of files. The BOM management process is in his or her head and buried in the details of an unknown number of hidden tabs on countless spreadsheets.*
> — "Using Excel for Bill of Materials (BOM) Management," Arena Solutions

With a BMMS, the search for product components is a simple query that can be performed across the entire BOM database in order to aggregate all of the components in the different products that will be required within certain time frames. The next step is to combine the forecast for each component by the number of components per BOM for all the BOMs in the BOM database, as represented by the formula below:

The Number of Final Products

X

The Number of Components Per Final Product

X

The Time Phased Forecast for the Final Product

=

The Total Component Demand Communicated to the Supplier

By providing the ability to perform this calculation quickly and with little effort, the BMMS helps the user to avoid missing any of the components, translating to an improved components forecast. The more comprehensive the unit estimate, the higher the number of units, the greater the negotiating leverage and the lower the price of each component. Therefore, the ability to easily obtain this information with queries on the BMMS results in lower costs to the company. In fact, a good BMMS will be able to show relationships in BOMs very naturally, as the "Where Used" view on the following page demonstrates:

The Arena "Where Used" view allows a user to quickly trace where a part is used across any BOM in the system. This showcases the strong associative linking within Arena Solutions. Finding associations like this in Arena Solutions is very natural, and does not require going to any special area within the application. The application allows a natural flow between the data elements.

Change Control in Spreadsheets

This case study is an excerpt from a paper by Arena Solutions. It is a story that has been repeated at many companies many times.

> *Phil kept his BOM in an Excel spreadsheet. It was an ornate thing; filled with colorful columns and hidden worksheets, complicated formulas, and the usual assortment of expected entries like purchasing order numbers and the dates Carlos could expect parts to arrive. The latter had a complementary column for actual arrive dates, quantities received, etc.—all the things a purchasing manager would care about. Phil was careful to save different revisions every time he made a change or updated information that Sue and Kyle sent him. That way, he knew which version was the last.*

He had a lot of different versions because he received daily updates from Kyle and Sue as they kept working. Kyle in particular was moving fast. He kept his electrical BOM as an Excel spreadsheet and every morning when he arrived he'd boot up Excel and select "Rev A" from his recent documents list, minimize it, and then update the data on the fly throughout the day as he added new parts, removed old ones, changed quantities on orders, and made various other changes.

The basic problem at Ellerby Manufacturing was that everybody— electrical, mechanical and purchasing—had by necessity, his or her own BOM dedicated to his or her department needs. Each department manipulated, revised and controlled its BOMs in isolation, but when it came time to merge all the BOMs into a releasable version, everything fell apart.

— "The Arena Solutions Guide to Outsourcing: Removing Barriers,
Maintaining Boundaries," Arena Solutions, 2011

Obviously, the design described in the case study above is a recipe for disaster. The design depends too heavily upon the capabilities of the person building the spreadsheet, and only a few people in the company have mastery over all the functions in the various spreadsheets. It is also rare for these types of spreadsheets to be documented by their creators, meaning that the company runs the risk of ending up with a solution that is essentially a software application, but one without a user manual. When a BMMS is used, the functionality is documented and online help is provided.

BOM Archival in Spreadsheets

A BOM can exist in many states or in different lifecycle stages. Different parts of the company focus on BOMs that are in different stages. Typically the supply chain departments are concerned with active BOMs, while design and engineering are concerned with new products, revisions to current products, or in leveraging the previous BOMs in order to create new BOMs. However, the number of BOMs can increase very rapidly; when a change is made to a BOM and the previous version of the BOM is retained, two BOMs now exist where previously there was one.

BOMs are storehouses for all manner of product information. They are a corporate asset where various versions of the BOM are maintained and a library of product information is created, along with the ability to manage this information. Old BOMs may be leveraged to make new products, but this strategy presents two challenges, especially to spreadsheets: The old BOM must be archived and held for what could be a long time, and it is difficult to predict when it may be useful to serve as a template for a future design. Inactive BOMs take up a lot of space in spreadsheets, but not only the old BOMs are kept: all the revised versions are stored as well. With spreadsheets, or any tool for which BOM management is inefficient, it is natural to want to purge the inactive BOMs to make the spreadsheet more manageable. One solution is to maintain the inactive BOMs in different spreadsheet versions, meaning that to find specific inactive BOMs, it is necessary to open multiple copies of old versions of the BOM spreadsheet and perform a search for the BOM in question. The upshot is that it is very unlikely that the BOM archive of a company without a BMMS will be as complete and achieve the same quality as that of a company with a BMMS.

Associated Documents of the BOM Spreadsheet

When one looks only at direct software expense, spreadsheets were an inexpensive tool, and were one of the few tools available to those that worked with BOMs prior to the existence of BOM software. The explanation of how spreadsheets have been used for the BOM has been slightly oversimplified in this chapter; in fact, other files were used in addition to spreadsheets. Specifications, which were tied to specific parts in the BOM, would be held in Word documents or PDF documents. CAD files in their native format, as well as exported image files that could be read by anyone (not just a person with say, a copy of SolidWorks), were necessary as well. Therefore, while a spreadsheet showed the BOM line items, the entirety of the BOM would be represented by a file folder. The spreadsheet showed the overall organizing logic of the BOMs and helped users to find other files in the file folder by declaring the file names in the spreadsheet. Sharing the

BOM required that not only the spreadsheet be shared, but that the associated files be sent as well (embedding files into a spreadsheet, particularly large files, is one of the best ways to drastically slow them down and cause them to crash). Since the entire file folder archive could not be sent, this meant hunting through the comprehensive BOM file folder to find the associated documents to send in addition to the spreadsheet—a manual and inefficient process and one which is essentially automated by the BMMS.

The One Real Use for BOMs in Spreadsheets: The Arena Part Saver

While I have spent much of this chapter proposing that spreadsheets are not a good technology for managing BOMs, they do in fact have an important place in the BOM development process, and this is when the design engineers are "shopping" for parts on various websites. Arena has a plug-in that allows items to be quickly and easily added from websites to a spreadsheet. The parts spreadsheet is then added to the Arena application.

This solution is designed for the engineer who is involved in the design process. As pointed out by Josh Robbins at Arena Solutions, engineers currently use spreadsheets to manage this process. They go to distributor websites to find parts that fit their design and then copy and paste every field into the spreadsheet, which is, of course, very tedious. With Parts List, they can go to one distributor after another and create the parts list.

Arena enables better BOM and part management through its Arena application, through its PDX viewer and also through its Part Saver. The Part Saver is a browser bookmark add-in that allows those searching for parts to automatically add them to a Google Spreadsheet. The addition of the bookmark is very simple: Go to http://www.arenasolutions/partsaver and drag the "Save to Parts List" link to the bookmark bar, as shown in the screenshot on the following page:

Now that the bookmark link has been added, it can be used with any compliant part website.

Here we are on a part page, and to add it, we simply need to select the bookmark that we just added. We can add comments and information to other fields, and then select the green "Save to Google Docs" button.

Arena PartSaver
for Google Docs

Heads up! Arena PartSaver is about to create a spreadsheet in your Google Docs account called:

☐ Arena Parts List

In order to do this, **we need you to grant access to your Google Docs account** so we can save your parts as rows in this spreadsheet.

On the next page, **you'll need to click Grant Access**.

Note: You may need to log in to your Google account first.

Go to Google permission page   By clicking this button, you agree to our Terms of Service.

When doing this for the first time, it's important to authenticate so you give permission to connect to Google Docs.

Now, we can see what it looks like in Google Docs. I have added two other parts to this spreadsheet using the same Part Saver link. This spreadsheet can eventually be imported into Arena Solutions.

Add Parts to Arena Parts List with Arena Part Saver

One way to use Arena Parts List is to save parts to a spreadsheet. However, another way is to save to the Arena Parts List web interface. Both processes work in much the same way. However, when complete, the parts can be very easily exported to a PDX, as shown in the following screenshots.

Arena PartsList

Parts List allows an electrical engineer to seamlessly document their prototype BOM.

Now the engineer will check various distributor websites for the right parts. Again, they will add the part by selecting the Part Saver link. This graphic is from Arena Solutions.

Now the part will be added to the Parts List, which is already open in another tab of the browser.

		Item Number	Manufacturer No.	Manufacturer	Description	Distributor	Distributor No
1	☑		BQ500110	Texas Instruments	Wireless Power Dedicated Digital Controller	Mouser	
2	☑		TCPT1300X01	Vishay Semiconductors	Photointerruptors Transmissive Optical Sensor	Mouser	782-TCPT1300
3	☑		Si5xx-PROG-EVB	Silicon Labs	Clock & Timer Development Tools I2C Programmable Evaluation Kit	Mouser	634-SI5XX-PR EVB
4	☑		A1302EUA-T	ALLEGRO MICROSYSTEMS	Hall Effect Sensor 10mA 5 Volt 3-Pin Ultra Mini SIP Bulk	Jameco	1718743
5	☑		CTRC-1330(B)	JAMECO VALUEPRO	EMI,SUPRESSION CORE,ROUND,BLKWITH CASE,.89 ODx.51 IDx1.42 L	Jameco	2094979
6	☑		H2852-R	JAMECO VALUEPRO	HIGH CLASS ABS PLASTIC SPEEDY BOXES	Jameco	18906
7	☑		19154-0004	Molex	InsulKrimp™ Butt Splice for 18-22 AWG Wire	Molex	
8	☑		55456-0559	Molex	1.25mm Pitch Mi II™ System Wire-to-Board Header, Single Row, Right Angle, SMT, 5 Circuits, with Plastic Peg, Lead-Free	Molex	

The part can then be exported to a PDX file, and then imported to Arena PDX.

The PDX, once complete, can then be sent to a contract manufacturer.

Conclusion

Spreadsheets used to manage the BOM are developed in an ad hoc manner. At this point, there is a lot of history regarding what happens when companies rely upon spreadsheets for BOM management, and it's not positive. In return for not viewing the BOM as the strategic entity that it is, companies that use spreadsheets must accept a very low level of BOM management functionality. Most companies don't realize the great disadvantage they are at against companies that have made a more informed choice and have stopped relying upon spreadsheets for BOM management. As pointed out by Arena Solutions, "The modern product record often includes a complex set of hundreds to thousands of structured items." A spreadsheet is not designed to manage this type of data. The limitations of spreadsheets for managing BOMs were listed earlier in this chapter. However, regardless of these limitations, and inappropriateness of spreadsheets for the task at hand, they persist as BOM management tools at many companies.

The problem is also one of scale. I can create new BOMs and place them in a spreadsheet quite easily. When the numbers of BOMs are limited, spreadsheets seem to be a reasonable tool to manage the information. On small spreadsheets, it's not much of a problem to find line items. When the identifiers are unique and consistent, filters can be applied to even large spreadsheets to find items. However, a spreadsheet solution will not scale with regard to consistency or "find-ability." Line items often contain information that is not consistent, particularly in spreadsheets that do not enforce change rules or apply consistency to how changes are managed. BOM line items can be copied or placed into the spreadsheet, including those items containing identical components to items already in the spreadsheet under different names. This will, of course, reduce the ability to find identical parts. However, it's important to be able to perform queries on the BOM database so that information can be provided to the supplier base, in addition to fulfilling the company's own internal information needs.

Spreadsheets can allow for various BOMs to be coded with different validity dates; however, keeping a large number of inactive BOMs in a spreadsheet can often cause the spreadsheet to become unwieldy. As a result, inactive BOMs tend to get "purged" and saved only in previous versions of BOM spreadsheets. One requirement for BOM management is a high degree of change control, something that spreadsheets lack. The Arena Solutions case study presented in this chapter illustrated this very well. Spreadsheets place the responsibility for effective change control and quality control on the users of the spreadsheet and offer few automatic protections that allow the company to enforce its rules with respect to what is changed and who changes it. In essence, the company relies upon the spreadsheet's users for all quality control, and they are taking this risk with a prized asset, something they probably would think twice about if spreadsheet solutions had not simply grown holistically. In fact, because so many people work on the BOM, and so many people have different authorization levels, BOM management requires a high degree of authorization control and requires a sophisticated, capable and nuanced authorization model. Spreadsheets have nothing like this.

Not only must a BOM management system maintain current BOMs and BOMs that are in development as new products, but must also serve as an archival system for all BOMs that the company chooses to keep. (Of course, some BOMs may be considered unusable in the future, and may be deleted; however, what can seem unusable one year can appear usable in another year.) However, most companies do not take this long-term view with respect to the BOM and BOM archival. Without making a spreadsheet unwieldy, the only good way to make a BOM archive is to save a version of the master BOM spreadsheet, and then place this saved version of the spreadsheet and all of its associated documents into an archive folder. This task needs to be performed on a periodic basis as new BOMs build up. During each new save, different BOMs can then be purged from the current master BOM file. However, there is no way around the fact that for those companies that use a spreadsheet to maintain their BOMs (along with a file folder of associated BOM files such as PDFs and JPEGs), companies are limited in their BOM archival capabilities, their BOM management and their BOM efficiency, and finding old BOMs to leverage for new products is a time-consuming process. Whenever a company uses a spreadsheet as its primary BOM management system, the overall BOM database and archive is reduced in value as a company asset.

While BOMs are often spoken of as being managed in spreadsheets, this is an oversimplification of what happens in reality. While the BOM's connection logic, and naming and numbering information, is contained or modeled in a spreadsheet, many other pieces of related information necessary to understanding the BOM in its totality are kept in different files and different file formats. The user then simply uses the spreadsheet as an index to find the names of these associated files. All of this is a great deal of overhead and maintenance. While the tools to manage a BOM this way are either free or very inexpensive, the costs in time and inefficiency are quite significant.

The Bill of Materials in ERP and External Planning Systems

To better understand the BOM as it is used in ERP systems, it is beneficial to walk through the planning process. Planning can be performed simply in an ERP system, or in a more complex manner with an external planning system. I cover the BOM in external planning systems in Chapter 6: "The Bill of Materials in External Planning Systems." Some companies only have an ERP system and do not use an external planning system. Where both an ERP system and an external planning system exist within a company, many of the planning functions that are usually performed in ERP are performed in the planning system.

From EBOM to MBOM

The manufacturing BOM or MBOM is created in the ERP system, and is a result of the engineering BOM (EBOM). As has been discussed previously, the EBOM *precedes* the MBOM because a product must be designed before it can be manufactured. ERP vendors designed their BOMs to support accounting, manufacturing and procurement and not much else. MBOMs are far more static and far less interactive than required by the engineering BOMs and only store text information, meaning that a great deal of information is left behind once a BOM transitions from design to manufacturing and supply chain. Therefore, it is not at all surprising that Arena Solutions, a leader in BMMS software, came out of the design area rather than the more limited (from a BOM perspective) manufacturing or ERP area. In fact, BOMs have changed very little since they were introduced in ERP systems such as SAP and Oracle. Arena has itself observed this fact, and has the following to say:

> *Without extensive customization, MRP/ERP systems typically also fall short on aggregation; their user interface is cumbersome and geared toward manufacturing and purchasing departments, not engineering. As a result, the creators of product data find it extremely difficult to maintain a current representation of the product in these systems during development. This is a natural result of the fact that a design goal of MRP/ERP systems is to limit the changes to product definition data that can be very expensive during production when inventory has already been stocked. This lack of flexibility renders these tools unsuitable for use during product development because they discourage alteration of product data—the very function of design.*
>
> — "The Arena Solutions Guide to Outsourcing: Removing Barriers, Maintaining Boundaries," Arena Solutions, 2011

Because design and engineering have such high requirements for their BOMs, I would say that people on the supply chain side of the company have a much more difficult time appreciating the functionality required for EBOMs than the other way around. The conversations I have had with design and engineering people demonstrate to me that their knowledge level with respect to the BOM and BOM technologies is simply much more advanced than that exhibited in similar discussions with supply chain professionals. I say this as a supply chain professional myself with no design background. Therefore, while a BMMS is all-encompassing of supply chain requirements, the more advanced functionality within the BMMS is really designed for engineering.

BOMs as implemented in ERP systems are increasingly dated and based upon a time when design, engineering, manufacturing and supply chain were all performed by one company at one location. ERP systems are by design, focused internally. Generally speaking, people do not log in to the ERP system of another company, and the ERP system interacts with systems external to the company primarily through transactions such as purchase orders. In today's environment, functions previously performed in-house are increasingly spread out across multiple companies, and ERP systems do not work very well in this environment. Furthermore, ERP BOMs have stayed static, even as the BOM functionality in the engineering and design side of the business has drastically improved. At this point, a BOM that is adjusted and reviewed by internal employees only is really an anachronism in an environment where engineering, design and manufacturing is spread out among many companies. BOMs today need to be highly collaborative to enable the work that needs to be done. Never before has maintaining BOMs in ERP systems or spreadsheets been so out of touch with what is happening in business. Arena Solutions makes the following observation:

In fact, a BMMS can help mitigate many of the weaknesses of ERP systems by connecting them to some of the most collaborative supply chain systems that have been designed, allowing each system to do what it is best at and share information through integration.

The Fields in the SAP ERP BOM

I have worked with ERP systems since 1997, I know the BOM in ERP systems to be an extremely limited master data object. Until I became exposed to the design and engineering side of the business, and began testing BMMS applications, I too thought that the BOM representation in ERP systems was "correct."

In the SAP ERP system (called R/3 or ECC), the following fields are part of the BOM. However, itemizing the list this way provides an inaccurate perspective on how much information is contained in most ERP BOMs. For this reason, I have marked the commonly filled-in fields with an "x."

1. Material (x)

2. Plant (x)

3. Alternative BOM (x)

4. Item Number (x)

5. Component (x)

6. Item Category (x)

7. Item ID (x)

8. Quantity (x)

9. Unit Of Measure (x)

10. Operation scrap in %

11. Component scrap in %

12. Co-product

13. AltItemGroup

14. Recurs. allowed

15. RecursiveCAD

16. IndicatorALE

17. IndicatorLead time offsetOper.

18. TL offset

19. Distribution Key

20. Phantom item

21. Special procurement

22. Engineering/design (o)

23. Production relevant (o)

24. Spare part indicator

25. Relevant to sales (o)

26. CostingRelevancy (o)

27. Material Prov Ind

28. Bulk Material

29. Bulk Mat.Ind.Mat.Mst

30. Prod. stor. locatin

31. Prodn Supply Area

32. Validity to (x)

33. Validity from (x)

Some fields that do not exist in the design and engineering system are incorporated in the MBOM. The *plant* field is one example; the necessity to designate a BOM per plant creates more copies of the BOM in the ERP system. Furthermore, both ERP systems and external planning systems have the concept of alternate BOMs. This is clear from the *Alternative BOM* field in the listing above. Priorities are assigned to the alternate BOMs to allow the system to select between them.

Each alternate BOM in the plant could be specific to a production line because the consumption of the components may change depending upon the setting of the machines, lot sizes, and the production process. Many ERP systems and planning systems have a separate master data object, which is the combination of a specific BOM, specific routing and specific work center/resource. Many of parent master data objects are necessary to represent all of the different combinations of the child master data objects. The graphic on the following page shows the logical connection between the BOM, routing and resource, and this parent master data object.

BOMs, Routings and Work Centers and the PPM and PDS

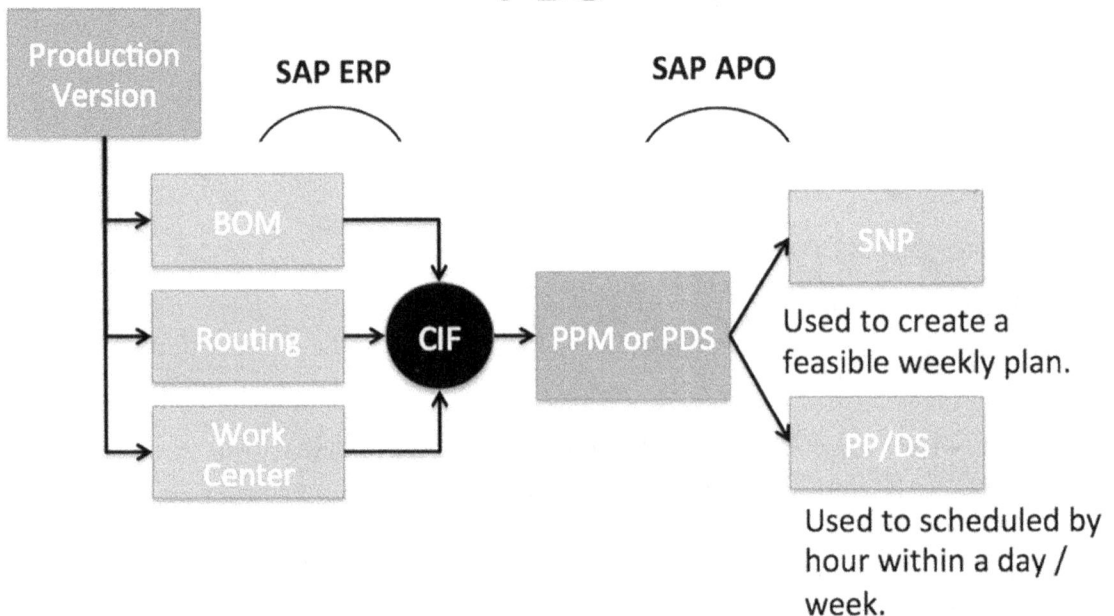

Background on Resources in SNP Versus PP/DS

PPMs and PDSs and their interaction with SNP and PP/DS is a common source of questions on APO (SAP's advanced planning software) projects. In fact, it's quite common for me to arrive on projects to find that the previous consultants had explained little about the PPM or PDS. This is one reason I created the article on how to decide between the PPM and PDS. However, even after selecting one of these two options, people still have a number of questions with respect to how either the PPM or PDS works with SNP and PP/DS.

http://www.scmfocus.com/sapplanning/2009/04/24/pds-vs-ppm-and-implications-for-bom-and-plm-management/

Common Questions on the PPM and PDS

The first question that usually arises is: *"How will the BOMs, work centers and routings in SAP ERP come across to APO?"* The answer is the combination of them, (i.e., what is a Production Version in SAP ERP becomes either a PPM or a PDS in APO). This basic connection between the different objects in the system is shown in the previous graphic.

The second question is: *"Will the work center resource be different in the SNP or PP/DS PPM or PDS?"* The answer to this is that APO allows the creation of a direct copy of any PPM from the SNP PPM to a PP/DS PPM. Secondly, in the case of the PDS, both SNP PDS and PP/DS PPM are automatically created by APO. Therefore, they match, and the most sustainable solution is to use the same PPM or PDSs. However, this often leads to the next logical question which is how SNP and PP/DS use the PPM or PDS, and here there are important differences. I find the following quotations from SAP illuminating:

1. Since PP/DS plans in detail, the plans for the PP/DS sources of supply are more detailed than the plans for the SNP PPMs.

2. PP/DS plans take account of all PP/DS relevant components and resources. For SNP, you use PPMs with simpler PPM plans with which you only plan the critical activities and components.

3. If you plan using PPMs in PP/DS, you can define in the conversion settings that PP/DS adopts the sources of supply defined by SNP. When an SNP order is converted, the system therefore uses the PP/DS PPM defined by the SNP order for the PP/DS orders.

—SAP Help

Therefore, SNP and PP/DS do use the PPMs and PDSs for different purposes. In this way, the PPMs and PDSs can be seen to contain some data that is "unused" by each application. However, from the original BOMs, work centers and routings in SAP ERP the Production Version is created in SAP ERP, and from the Production Version the PPM or PDS is created in APO. However, this does not contradict the fact that creating both SNP and PP/DS PPMs and PDSs from the CIF (which connects ERP to APO) is an efficient mechanism to not only get the initial data from ERP, but also to repeatedly receive changes and updates from the ERP system.

PPMs and PDSs can be thought of as Production Versions from SAP ERP in APO. The logic for creating a master data object like this is that it allows a unique combination of BOM, routing and work center to be represented by an object. SAP has automated most of the process of creating the PPM and PDS so that companies that have ERP can just worry about creating their BOMs, routings and work centers correctly. The PPM provides more flexibility than the PDS because they can be altered in APO, and in some cases, (e.g., modeling supplier resources), a PPM must be used because no work centers or routings are allowed to exist in a vendor location. Therefore, it's important to define all of the company's needs in this area and then observe a flexible approach with respect to PPM and PDS selection.

ERP Production Version	APO PPM/PDS	BOM	Routing	Work Center	Resource Capacity	Priority Level
1	1	A	A	A	500	1
2	2	B	A	A	500	2
3	3	A	A	B	600	3

In SAP ERP, this master data object is called a production version. A screen shot of a production version is shown on the following page:

Production Version: Mass Processing

Selection Conditions

Plant	1000	Plant 1
Material	CH-1420	

			Task List Type	Group
MRP Controller	100	Detailed plng	Master Recipe ▼	MR-09001
Key date	07.06.2012	Rate-based plng	Master Recipe ▼	MR-09001
Production line	ASSEMBLY	Rough-Cut Plng	Master Recipe ▼	MR-09001

Produ...

Production line for repetitive manufacturing (1)

Work Center Category	Find by class	Name of work center	Tech...

Plant

Work center cat.

Plant

Work center

Description

Language Key   EN

Maximum No. of Hits   500

1000
1000
1000
1000
1000
1000
1000
1000
1000
1000
1000
1000
1000

SAP ERP connects to SAP APO, an advanced planning system, and the planning system also represents the production version master data object as its own master data object, which is either a PPM or PDS (clients have a choice which to use).

http://www.scmfocus.com/sapplanning/2012/07/27/the-connection-between-boms-routings-work-centers-in-erp-and-ppms-pdss-in-apo/

Multiple variations of BOMs in the ERP and planning system are frequently due to the quantities in the individual components. A product can be manufactured from alternative combinations of materials for a variety of reasons, such as the quantity produced (also known as the lot size) or how the processing equipment consumes the components on the BOM. These reasons might not normally occur to anyone without a manufacturing background.

In order to make the master data as manageable as possible, companies often try to standardize BOMs across the various plants. However, there are a number of natural variations which result in a proliferation of very similar BOMs, all of which require maintenance.

We discussed aspects of the list of fields in the SAP BOM, but have more to talk about. For your convenience, I have repeated the BOM field list below.

1. Material (x)

2. Plant (x)

3. Alternative BOM (x)

4. Item Number (x)

5. Component (x)

6. Item Category (x)

7. Item ID (x)

8. Quantity (x)

9. UOM (x)

10. Operation scrap in %

11. Component scrap in %

12. Co-product

13. AltItemGroup

14. Recurs. allowed

15. RecursiveCAD

16. IndicatorALE

17. IndicatorLead time offsetOper.

18. TL offset

19. Distribution Key

20. Phantom item

21. Special procurement

22. Engineering/design (o)

23. Production relevant (o)

24. Spare part indicator

25. Relevant to sales (o)

26. CostingRelevancy (o)

27. Material Prov Ind

28. Bulk Material

29. Bulk Mat.Ind.Mat.Mst

30. Prod. stor. locatin

31. Prodn Supply Area

32. Validity to (x)

33. Validity from (x)

The fields that I have marked with (o) indicate the variations of the original BOM in SAP, each of which indicates a different usage and must be maintained separately, They also represent how many different associated—but separately maintained—BOMs there will be in SAP for the original BOM. Each BOM usage designation has its own BOM number. This functionality exists because a BOM can be coded for different uses e.g., design, production, costing, and one of the major functionalities provided, according to SAP, is separate reporting based upon the BOM usage (called, not coincidentally "BOM Usage"). BOM usage does not add extra fields to the BOM, but instead allows the BOM to access different functionalities in SAP ERP. SAP refers to this as the "area of validity." They state the following with respect to the area of validity:

*You can use a material BOM to manage data that applies directly to production. This is why the area of validity is the plant. The plant is the location where all necessary work-scheduling procedures are organized, such as MRP and creating routings. In this case, you create a plant-specific BOM. However, you can also create a group BOM, **without** reference to a plant. For example, a designer maintains a group BOM during the design phase of a product, then the BOM is allocated to one or more plants for production purposes.*

The R/3 System allows you to maintain individual BOMs for any area of your company. These BOMs are maintained independently of each other and are assigned different internal BOM numbers. In this way, each area is only dealing with the specific data it requires. In Customizing for Production, define individual BOM usages for the different areas within your company by choosing.

Basic data → Bill of Material → General data → BOM usage → *Define BOM usages.*

Change material BOM: Initial Screen

Item

Material	H10
Plant	0001
BOM Usage	1
Alternative BOM	

Effectivity

Change Number	
Valid From	28.06.2012
Revision Level	

BOM Usage (1)   13 Entries found

Restrictions

Usa	Pro	Eng/d	P	Spa	Cost	Sal	Usage text
1	+	.	-	.	.	-	Production
2	.	+	-	.	.	.	Engineering/Design
3	.	.	-	.	.	.	Universal
4	-	-	+	.	.	-	Plant Maintenance
5	.	.	-	.	.	+	Sales and Distribution
6	.	.	-	.	+	.	Costing
7	.	-	-	.	.	.	Empties
8	-	.	-	-	.	-	Stability Study
9	+	.	-	.	.	-	Production Rework
C	-	-	+	.	.	-	Configuration Control
M	.	.	.	.	.	.	External Munitions Display
T	+	.	-	.	.	-	Production (Mixing)
Y	.	.	-	.	.	-	Production Rework EX Stock

13 Entries found

Here is what SAP has to say about some of the major BOM usage categories:

The design BOM includes all the components of the product and their technical data from the design point of view. This BOM is generally not linked to any order.

The production BOM includes all the items required from the production and assembly point of view. To assemble a product, you only require items that are relevant to production, which contain process data.

The costing BOM describes the product structure and is used to automatically determine the costs of the materials required for a product. Items that are not relevant to costing are not included in the costing BOM.

The BOM usage is in a way quite unusual, because creating an extra BOM usage type does not extend the BOM, but instead creates a duplicate BOM in the SAP ERP system.

However, playing off of the first paragraph of the quotation, while it is possible to create a design BOM, it is difficult to see why a company would create a BOM that is valid a design BOM in SAP ERP. A central assumption of SAP is that design and engineering work with the SAP ERP system, when in fact they do not. Statements such as these can make executives think that design and engineering can be expected to perform their work in SAP ERP and that the needs of design and engineering are covered, when in fact they are not.

Display material BOM: Item: All data

🖫 🖫 | Reference items 🍶 👤 Subitems | ✏ Long Text 🔁

Material	CH–1420	🗗 talyst (Grade A)
Plant	1000 Plant 1	
Alternative BOM	1	

Basic Data ‖ Status/Lng Text ‖ Administr. ‖ Document Assgmt

BOM item

Item Number	0020	
Component	CH–4110	Bag, 25 LB
Item Category	L Stock item	
Item ID	00000002	
Sort String		
☐ Sub-item ID		

Quantity Data

Quantity	7	EA	☐ Fixed quantity	
Operation scrap in %	0,00	☐ Net ID	Component scrap (%)	0,00

General Data

☐ Co-product   ☐ Recurs. allowed

AltItemGroup [ ]   ☐ Recursive

                      ☐ CAD Indicator

[Discontin. data]   ☐ ALE indicator

MRP Data

Lead-time offset	0
Oper. LT offset	0
Distribution key	
☐ Phantom item	

The following information is the "header" data. By selecting the "Subitems" button, one is taken to the material list. The material list shows the material association that makes up the BOM and has the following fields:

1. Item

2. Component

3. Component Description

4. Quantity

5. Unit of Measure

6. Valid From

7. Valid to

8. Item Category

9. Item IDs

10. Assembly

11. Sub Items

That is it. Those are all the fields available within SAP ERP for the BOM. If this seems extremely limited, especially to those with a background in design and engineering, you are correct; it is quite limited. In fact, only a small subset of the design and engineering BOM is required for supply chain planning and execution. Although some fields such as "plant" exist in the MBOM, they are not necessary in the EBOM. These are only text fields, and there is no ability to store any of the types of documents that we discussed in Chapter 3: "The Bill of Materials (EBOM) in the Design and Engineering Systems." Secondly— and this point is quite important and will be discussed again in Chapter 7: "The BOM Management System: The BMMS"— all BOM information is simply a subset of data that is kept in the BMMS.

Document Attachment to the BOM and the Material Master in SAP ERP

In SAP ERP, the BOM has a series of fields, listed above, that describe the BOM. In SAP ERP, documents (including CAD documents and other design and engineering documents) can be attached to either the BOM or to the components of the BOM, which is in the material master. The attachments can be performed in the Documents tab of the BOM, as shown in the screen shot below:

Creating an attachment to the material master is shown on the following page:

Change Material CH-1010 (Storage tank materials)

⇨ Additional Data   Org. Levels   Check Screen Data   🔒

| Basic data 1 | Basic data 2 | Classification | Purchasing | Foreign trade im... |

Material   CH-1010   Acrylic resin

General data

Base Unit of Measure	LB	US pound	Material Group	02
Old material number			Ext. Matl Group	YQ_BM_USER_EXIT
Division			Lab/Office	
Product allocation				
X-plant matl status			Valid from	
			GenItemCatGroup	

Selecting the Additional Data button will take you to the area of the Material Master interface where documents can be attached.

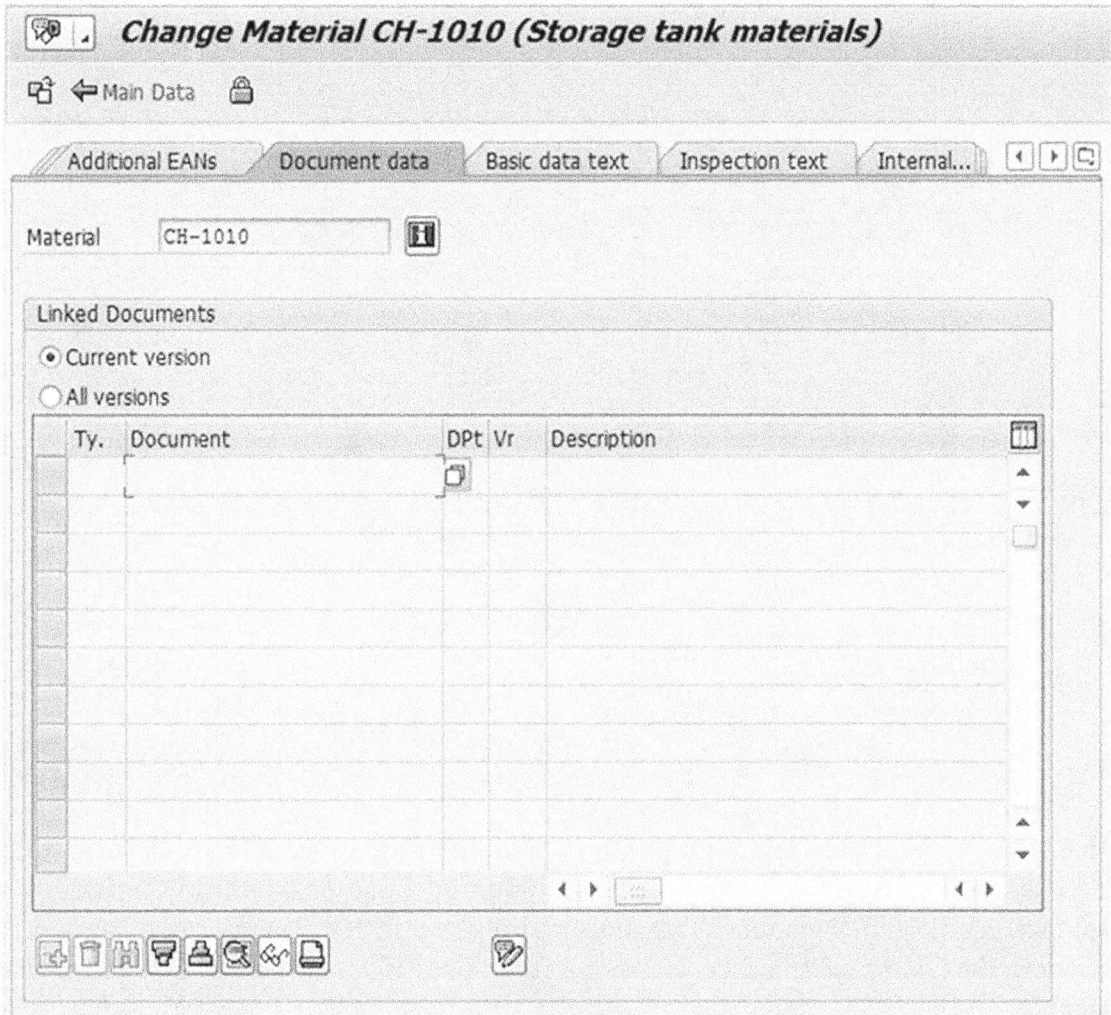

Once in this view, the button in the upper left corner can be selected to display the option to attach a document, which brings up the screen on the following page:

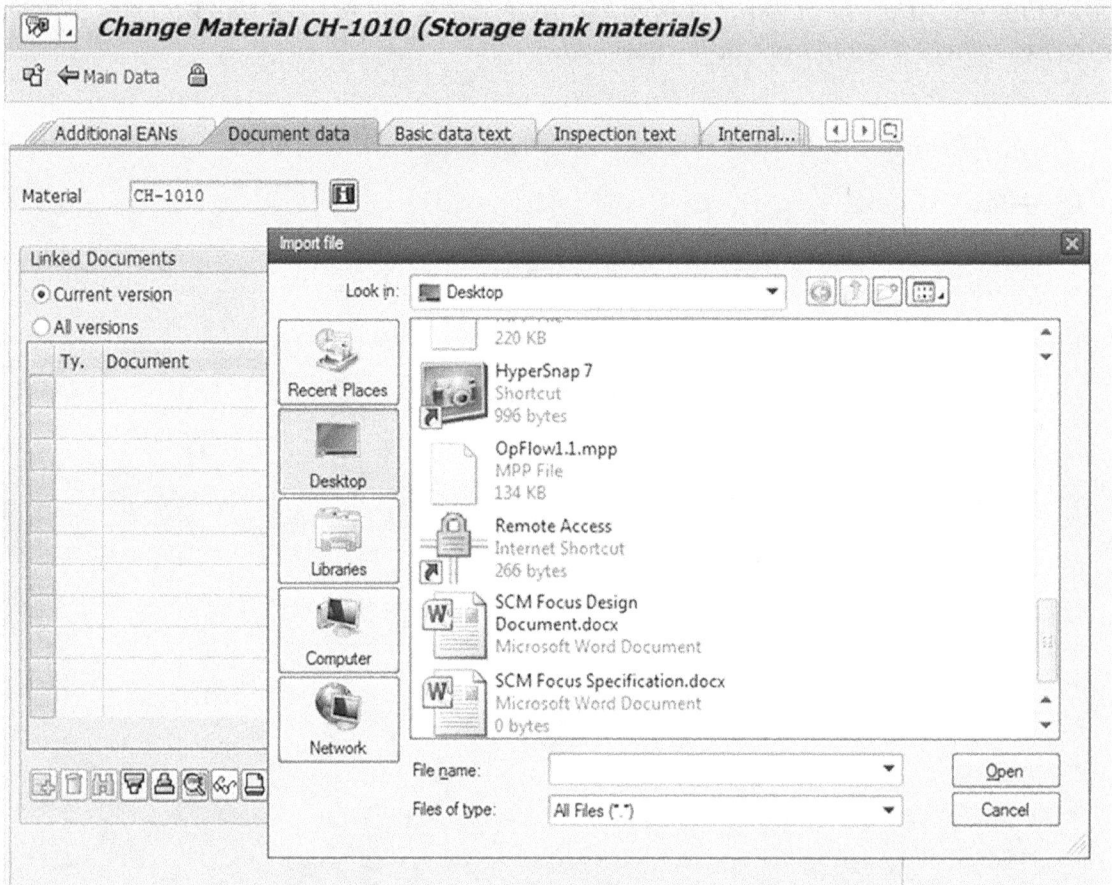

However, while attaching documents to a material master is often described in SAP documentation, in fact it is rarely done because design and engineering seldom use the ERP system. The material master in ERP is simply designed to support the ERP functionality; it is not a functional BOM interface that those who work with the BOM would use to interact with the BOM. Therefore, when this approach to managing documents is presented to executives of an implementing company, they might consider this function to be useful and to meet part of their requirements, when in fact it is not particularly useful to their employees. That is, it is unreasonable to expect someone to manage BOM design and engineering documents in SAP.

Variant BOMs

SAP can perform something called "variant configuration" — the ability to alter the configuration of the finished good— which is used in both make-to-order and assemble-to-order environments. Variant configuration requires a "master BOM" which describes the production process for each product variant. The logic of variant configuration essentially converts the production order into the specific components required for the configuration to meet the requirements of the product ordered. Variant BOMs are BOMs that are a change to the basic model. For instance, if parts are added or removed, or if a different number of parts (say two units of a part versus one unit of a part) are required to make a finished good, then it is necessary to create a variant BOM. Variant BOMs provide flexibility to a company, and are a relatively simple way to make adjustments to a pre-existing BOM. Variant BOMs are different from alternative BOMs, which occur when the only difference between the BOMs is the number of components, with no addition or deletion of components.

Product Structure

The product structure is a way of seeing a nested view of the BOM and associated information. In a similar way, there is something called the BOM Material Browser.

Item Categories

When a BOM is created, it is set up for something called an "item category." This category controls how the BOM is treated by SAP. These distinctions include the following:

- *Is a material number a required entry?*

- *Is the item to be checked against stock?*

- *Is the item a text-only item with no further functions?*

- *Are different-sized sections of the item to be entered?*

- *Are negative quantities allowed?*

- *Are sub-items supported?*

- *Is the item a plant maintenance (PM) structure element?*

- *Is the item an intra material?*

- *Is the item a document item or class item?*

- *Which screens are selected and which fields appear on the item detail screens?—SAP Help*

In the *Customizing for Production* function, you define the features of the item category. This is done by going to the SAP IMG (this is where basic configuration is performed) by choosing the following path:

Production → Basic Data → *Bill of Material* → *Item Data* → *Define item categories.*

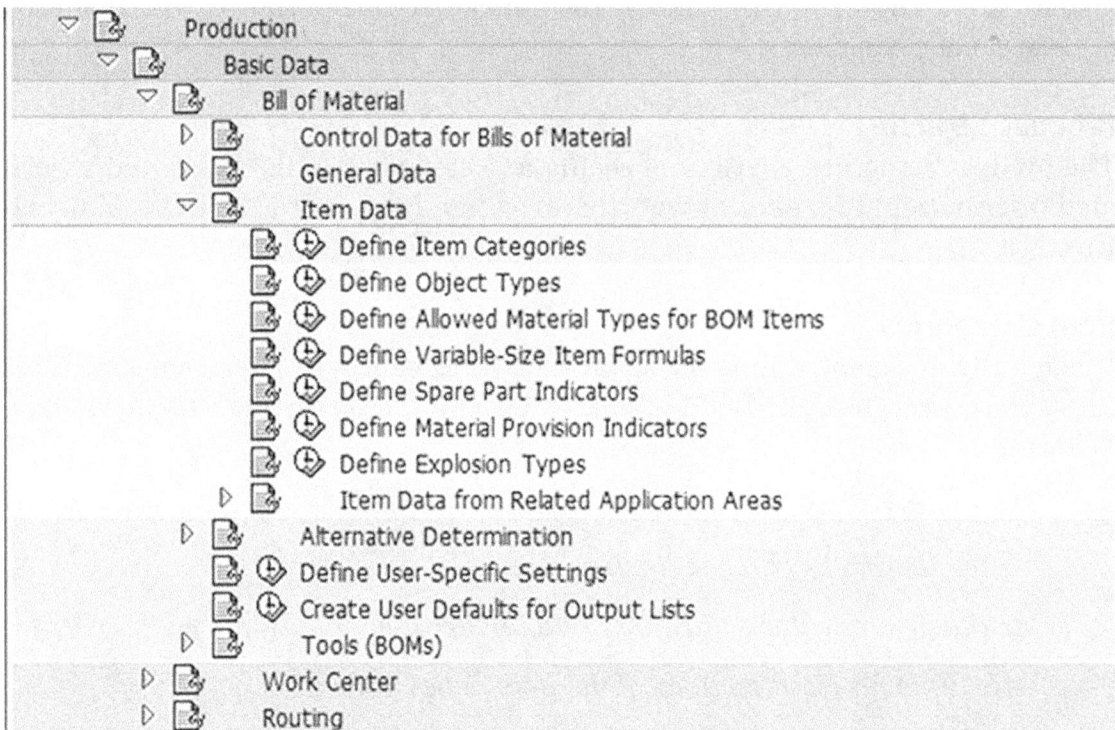

```
▽ 📄   Production
   ▽ 📄     Basic Data
      ▽ 📄       Bill of Material
         ▷ 📄         Control Data for Bills of Material
         ▷ 📄         General Data
         ▽ 📄         Item Data
              📄 ⊕       Define Item Categories
              📄 ⊕       Define Object Types
              📄 ⊕       Define Allowed Material Types for BOM Items
              📄 ⊕       Define Variable-Size Item Formulas
              📄 ⊕       Define Spare Part Indicators
              📄 ⊕       Define Material Provision Indicators
              📄 ⊕       Define Explosion Types
           ▷ 📄           Item Data from Related Application Areas
         ▷ 📄         Alternative Determination
              📄 ⊕       Define User-Specific Settings
              📄 ⊕       Create User Defaults for Output Lists
         ▷ 📄         Tools (BOMs)
      ▷ 📄       Work Center
      ▷ 📄       Routing
```

The available item categories are shown in the screen show below:

Change View "Item Categories": Overview

New Entries

ICt	MatInpt	InvMg	TxtItm	VSIte	DocItm	ClsItm	PM Str	IntraM	+/- Sign	SubI	ItmCtrl	Item category text
C	≠	☑☐	☐	☐	☐	☐	☐	☐	+	☑	0001	Compatible Unit
D	-	☐	☐	☐	☑	☐	☐	☐	+	☐	0001	Document item
I	+	☐	☐	☐	☐	☐	☑	☐	+	☑	0001	PM structure element
K	-	☐	☐	☐	☐	☑	☐	☐	+	☐	0001	Class item
L	+	☑	☐	☐	☐	☐	☐	☐	.	☑	0001	Stock item
M	+	☐	☐	☐	☐	☐	☐	☑	.	☐	0001	Intra material
N	.	☐	☐	☐	☐	☐	☐	☐	.	☑	0003	Non-stock item
R	+	☑	☐	☑	☐	☐	☐	☐	+	☑	0002	Variable-size item
T	-	☐	☑	☐	☐	☐	☐	☐	+	☐	0001	Text item

Intra Material

Plant Maintenance

Class Items

Document Items

Variable sized item

These item categories are defined as follows:

- Stock Items: When a component is planned to be kept in stock.

- Non stock Items: When an item is only procured for a specific production order.

- Variable-Sized Items: When the need is for differently-sized sections of material (often raw material) to be represented by material in the BOM.

- Plant Maintenance Items: Items used not for production but for plant maintenance.

- Intra Materials: Used for process industries, they are materials that only exist temporarily between two sub processes.

- Document Items: These are attached documents, often for design and engineering.

- Class Items: Used for configurable material.

The BOM and Subcontracting in SAP ERP

Subcontracting is the process of providing input products to a supplier, who then partially or completely manufacturers these inputs into a product. There are three major settings in SAP ERP to enable subcontracting:

1. Configure the BOMs for subcontracting (choose the subcontracting material as the header material, set the BOM explosion indicator).

2. Set up the Material Master for subcontracting (by selecting the Special Procurement Field in the MRP 2 tab).

3. Create an additional subcontracting purchasing info record by choosing the subcontractor category.

In order to perform subcontracting in SAP ERP alone or with SAP along with SAP APO (SAP APO has its own additional functionality which extends subcontracting with advanced planning), the BOM must be coded through the provision indicator as being either supplied by a customer or a vendor. As stated by SAP:

In Customizing, you define who provides the item for each material provision indicator by choosing Bill of Material → Item Data → Define material provision indicators. You set either the Material to be provided by customer indicator or the Material to be provided by vendor indicator. In material requirements planning (MRP), the system reads the material provision indicator. In BOM reporting functions, you can use this indicator as a selection criterion.

Only maintain this indicator for the BOM component if the material master record of the header material supports subcontracting (MRP data, field Special procurement). The special procurement key Subcontracting means that all components of the BOM are provided to the vendor for further processing. The items are copied to a subcontracting order.

*Items to be provided to the vendor must **not** contain the Material to be provided by vendor indicator.*

***Dependent requirements** are generated for these items. These items are in the subcontracting order as materials to be provided. Goods issue can be planned in advance using a reservation. In inventory management, a transfer posting is made for these components from unrestricted-use stock to vendor stock.*

- *Items that are already on the vendor's premises and that your company does not need to provide have the Material to be provided by vendor indicator.*

- ***No dependent requirements** are generated for these items.*

- *Subcontracting and Production Versions*

When processing a purchase document item (type subcontracting), the system determines the material BOM in accordance with the vendor you want to order from. These BOM versions of a material are stored in the material master as production versions. Individual production versions are linked to suppliers either in the quota arrangement or in the purchasing info record.

There are also several steps that are required to set up subcontracting functionality in SAP APO, which is covered in this article:

http://www.scmfocus.com/sapplanning/2012/05/27/sub-contracting/

Routing and Work Stations

In the ERP system, the BOM has a strong connection with the master data objects of the routing and the work centers. "Routing" is the sequence and processing of material through the production facility, while "work centers" are the equipment used to process the BOM into a finished product. These master data objects control the production planning for the product and are related holders of data. For instance, when SAP ERP is connected to SAP APO, the BOM, routing and work center come through an integration layer called the CIF, and are brought into SAP APO to create either a PPM or a PDS, both of which hold BOM, routing and work center data populated by SAP ERP.

The book, *Factory Physics,* includes the following quotation on work centers. I find the quote to be interesting and informative because of its broad definition of the work center. Rather than referring to the work center as one piece of equipment, *Factory Physics* defines it as an area of similar processing within a manufacturing facility:

> *A workstation is a collection of one or more machines or manual stations that perform (essentially) identical functions. Examples include a turning station made up of several vertical lathes, an inspection station made up of several benches staffed by quality inspectors, and a burn-in station consisting of a single room where components are heated for testing purposes. In process-oriented*

layouts, workstations are physically organized according to the operations they perform. Alternatively, in product-oriented layouts, they are organized in lines making specific products. The terms station, WorkCentre, and process center are synonymous with workstation.

Factory Physics also has the following to say on routings:

A routing describes the sequence of workstations passed through by a part. Routings begin at a raw material, component or subassembly stock point and end at either an intermediate stock point or finished goods inventory.

Again, *Factory Physics* defines the workstation as a grouping of similar or identical equipment. As such, the routing is the flow between similar processing areas. Combining physical work centers into virtual work centers (work centers that are placed into the model) keeps the model as simple as possible and reduces the amount of master data maintenance, while still representing and modeling the work centers accurately.

Therefore, ERP's emphasis with regard to the BOM is simply to "connect the dots" of what is necessary to bring the materials into the manufacturing plant, showing which work centers the materials will be routed through in order to complete their manufacture. When one considers all the other issues that we have discussed with respect to the BOM, it should be apparent how limited the ERP system's view of the BOM is. It is perfectly fine for the ERP system to take this limited view, but this can never be the overall company's view of the BOM.

Subcomponent Lead Times

To integrate the BOM information within the BMMS with the ERP system requires that a subset of the BOM information—essentially only those elements that are important to manufacturing— be taken from the BMMS. In effect, the MBOM is "dumbed down" into what I call a mini-BOM. Once a BOM is manufactured, an enormous amount of information that was necessary for the EBOM is no longer relevant. For a finished good, manufacturing and procurement want to know the number of subcomponent line items and what qualities of each subcomponent line item are necessary to manufacture the product. The ERP or planning system also needs to know the lead times of each subcomponent so it can order the items far enough in advance for them to all arrive in time for assembly. The lead times are stored not in the MBOM, but in each individual product file. Therefore, information that is stored in the BMMS for each BOM is also broken apart and stored in different master data objects in the supply chain systems. By performing lead time estimation, and in negotiating lead times with suppliers (for instance, offering better terms for guarantees of specific lead times), the design and engineering process can help make the product easier to manufacture. Once the lead times are set in the BMMS, they can be managed smoothly by the ERP system, and as time progresses these lead times are supposed to be updated on a periodic basis to reflect the actual lead times. However, the BMMS also contains the lead times. This is again interesting as the lead times are not part of the BOM.

Exploring the SAP BOM User Interface

The SAP BOM interface is extremely limited such that it can be shown in just a few screenshots. I have been working with SAP for some time, and the SAP BOM functionality remains relatively static. Hopefully the following screenshots will demonstrate to you that you should not count on manipulating or otherwise managing your BOMs in SAP ERP. Rather, you want to do all the work in an external system and then simply populate the necessary fields in the SAP BOM through an interface. In fact, I suggest comparing and contrasting the screenshots on the following page with the numerous screenshots of Arena Solutions provided throughout this book, and visualizing what it might be like to manage the BOM information in each system.

The following screenshots show the SAP BOM interface:

Display material BOM: Item: All data

Reference items   Subitems   Long Text

Material	CH-1420	talyst (Grade A)
Plant	1000 Plant 1	
Alternative BOM	1	

Basic Data | **Status/Lng Text** | **Administr.** | **Document Assgmt**

BOM Item

Item Number	0020
Component	CH-4110 Bag, 25 LB
Item Category	L Stock item
Item ID	00000002

Administrative Data

Created on	05.07.2012	By	502105023
Changed on		by	

Validity Periods

Valid From	Valid to	Change No.	Chg No. To	DeID	Effect. type	
05.07.2012	31.12.9999			☐		

Display material BOM: Item: All data

🖫 🖫 | Reference Items 🖨 ⚖ Subitems   ✏ Long Text   ⚚

Material   CH-1420   📋 talyst (Grade A)
Plant   1000 Plant 1
Alternative BOM   1

| Basic Data | Status/Lng Text | Administr. | Document Assgmt |

BOM Item

Item Number	0020
Component	CH-4110 Bag, 25 LB
Item Category	L Stock item
Item ID	00000002

Item Text

Line 1
Line 2

Item Status

☐ Engineering/design
☑ Production relevant
☐ Plant maintenance
Spare part indicator
Relevant to sales
CostingRelevncy   X

Further Data

Mat. Provision Ind.
☐ Bulk Material
☐ Bulk Mat.Ind.Mat.Mst
Prod. stor. location
Prodn Supply Area

Change material BOM: General Item Overview

🖩 🖩 🗔 🖨 👤Subitems	New entries 🗑 ⋐ 🗐Header 📄Validity

Material   CH-1420   Catalyst (Grade A)
Plant   1000 Plant 1
Alternative BOM   1

Material	Document	General

Item	ICt	Document	Ty.	DPt	Vr	Component description	Valid From	Valid to	
0010	L					Bag, 10 LB	05.07.2012	31.12.9999	
0020	L					Bag, 25 LB	05.07.2012	31.12.9999	
0030									

Surprisingly, that is it. The functionality has the following characteristics:

1. The association between all of the materials that are part of the BOM is shown in the BOM Material tab. The list is not indented to show the hierarchy of the BOM. The hierarchy must be determined by reading the description of the "component" or material that is in the list.

2. The interface is designed for access by internal employees and has no web interface. In any case, because this data is used by the ERP system to generate its output, you would never want external parties to be able to access these screens.

It is interesting to consider the things that one does not think about with respect to the BOM when one comes from the ERP or an external planning environment. One such example is the ability to perform a query across BOMs. BOM functionality in ERP and external planning systems do not support this query. A BOM can be copied to create a new BOM and individual BOMs can be reviewed, but development for ERP or external planning systems is not focused on managing across the various BOMs. While it is always possible to write a custom report, none of the associative linking or cross-comparison functionality that is in a BMMS exists in SAP ERP. This is, of course, very limiting for the companies that rely upon ERP and external planning systems to make adjustments to the BOM. Compare and contrast this to the view of the BOM in Arena Solutions' BMMS.

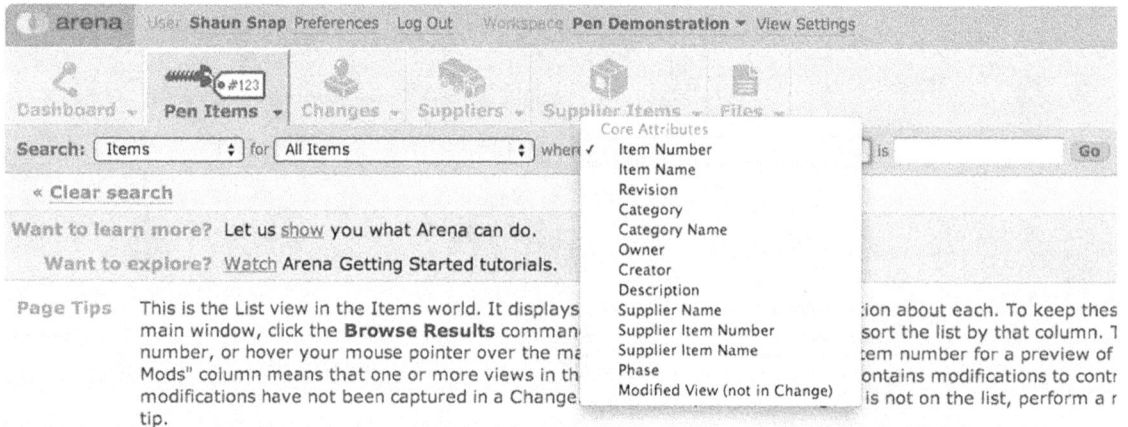

Arena allows for searches by many attributes.

Here we searched for every item that had the word "barrel" in its item name. Notice that part names were found that did not contain the word "barrel." For example, when we check the pen shaft, we find that it is associated with the part that includes "barrel" in its item name. This type of association is very difficult to replicate in a spreadsheet.

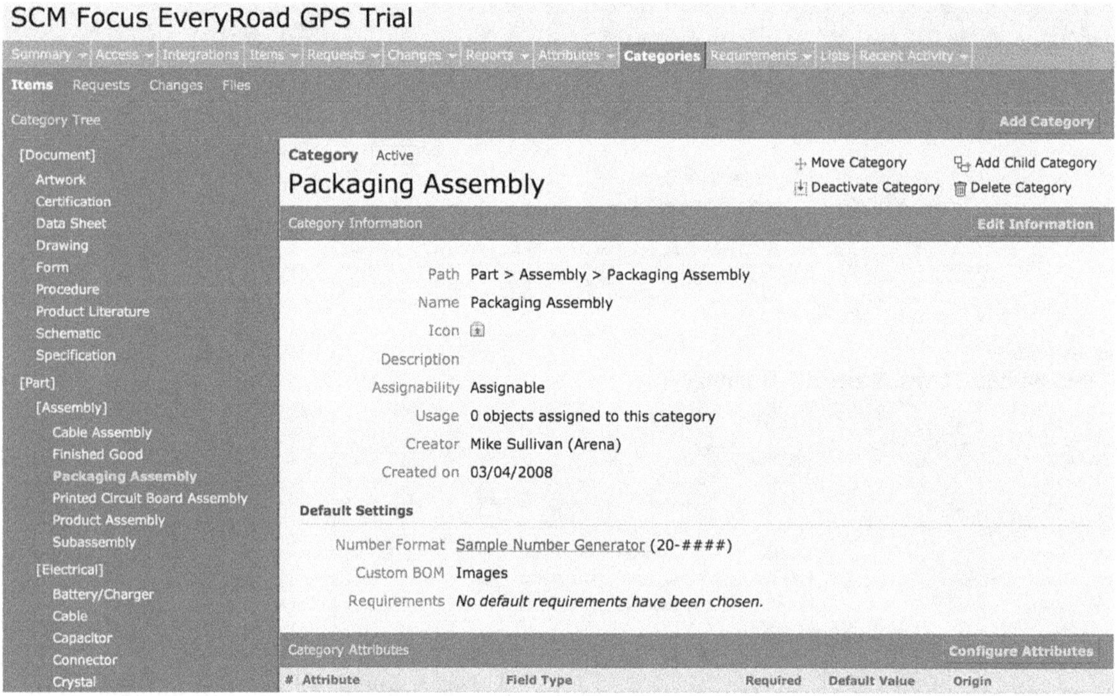
SCM Focus EveryRoad GPS Trial
Summary Access Integrations Items Requests Changes Reports Attributes Categories Requirements Lists Recent Activity
Items Requests Changes Files
Category Tree
Add Category
[Document]
Artwork
Certification
Data Sheet
Drawing
Form
Procedure
Product Literature
Schematic
Specification
[Part]
[Assembly]
Cable Assembly
Finished Good
Packaging Assembly
Printed Circuit Board Assembly
Product Assembly
Subassembly
[Electrical]
Battery/Charger
Cable
Capacitor
Connector
Crystal
Category Active
Packaging Assembly
Move Category
Add Child Category
Deactivate Category
Delete Category
Category Information
Edit Information
Path Part > Assembly > Packaging Assembly
Name Packaging Assembly
Icon
Description
Assignability Assignable
Usage 0 objects assigned to this category
Creator Mike Sullivan (Arena)
Created on 03/04/2008
Default Settings
Number Format Sample Number Generator (20-####)
Custom BOM Images
Requirements No default requirements have been chosen.
Category Attributes
Configure Attributes
Attribute
Field Type
Required
Default Value
Origin

Notice how the part in this BOM is categorized. The breadcrumbs at the top of the screen show that it belongs to Assembly and then to the level below called Packaging Assembly.

Details for

SCM Focus EveryRoad GPS Trial

Summary ▾ | Access ▾ | Integrations | Items ▾ | Requests ▾ | Changes ▾ | Reports ▾ | Attributes ▾ | **Categories** | Requirements ▾ | Lists | Recent Activity ▾

Items   Requests   Changes   Files

Category Tree   **Add Category**

[Document]
  Artwork
  Certification
  Data Sheet
  Drawing
  Form
  Procedure
  Product Literature
  Schematic
  Specification
[Part]
  [Assembly]
    Cable Assembly
    Finished Good
    Packaging Assembly
    Printed Circuit Board Assembly
    Product Assembly
    Subassembly
  [Electrical]
    Battery/Charger
    Cable
    Capacitor
    Connector

Category   Active   ⊹ Move Category   ⧉ Add Child Category

Drawing   ↧ Deactivate Category   🗑 Delete Category

Category Information   **Edit Information**

Path	Document > Drawing
Name	Drawing
Icon	📄
Description	
Assignability	Assignable
Usage	0 objects assigned to this category
Creator	Michael Sullivan
Created on	12/01/2008

Default Settings

Number Format	Sample Number Generator (90-####)
Custom BOM	Sample Custom BOM
Requirements	*No default requirements have been chosen.*

Category Attributes   **Configure Attributes**

To find any drawings with the part tree, one simply selects a different menu item to the left.

	#	Item Number	Item Name	Category	Phase	Wkg Mods	Where Used		Files	Rqmts	Qty	BOM Notes / Ref Des
▶	1	20-0003 rev A	EveryRoad, Front Bezel Assembly	Subassembly	In Prod	⚠ ▾	▾		2 ▾	✔ ▾	1 each	
▼	2	20-0004 rev B	EveryRoad, Rear Assembly	Subassembly	In Prod		▾		2 ▾	✖ ▾	1 each	
▼	1	20-0015 rev B	EveryRoad, PCBA, Model 300	Printed Circuit Board Assembly	In Prod		▾		6 ▾	✖ ▾	1 each	
	1	40-0035 rev A	EveryRoad, Circuit Board	Printed Circuit Board	In Prod		▾		2 ▾	? ▾	1 each	
	2	40-0038 rev A	GPS Micro controller	Misc. Electrical	In Prod		▾		2 ▾	? ▾	1 each	U2
	3	40-0039 rev A	USB Connector	Connector	In Prod		▾		4 ▾	✔ ▾	1 each	J4
	4	40-0041 rev A	0.1uF Ceramic Chip Capacitor	Capacitor	In Prod	⚠ ▾	▾		7 ▾	✔ ▾	5 each	C15, C6, C10-12
	5	40-0042 rev A	10k Resistor	Resistor	In Prod	⚠ ▾	▾		3 ▾	✖ ▾	8 each	R1, R5, R11, R12, R14, R16, R23, R24
	6	40-0043 rev A	1k Resistor	Resistor	In Prod		▾		4 ▾	✔ ▾	4 each	R25, R38, R31, R32
	7	40-0044 rev A	1.0uF Ceramic Capacitor, 1206	Capacitor	In Prod		▾		4 ▾	? ▾	1 each	C3
	8	40-0045 rev A	Low-dropout 5.0V 100mA Voltage Regulator	Misc. Electrical	In Prod	⚠ ▾	▾		1 ▾	✖ ▾	1 each	VR1

Notice how the basic bill of material view is shown above. There is significant nesting, which means that the header items can be selected to display more detail.

The Bill of Material and MRP

The BOM is really at the heart of the supply and production planning procedure called material requirements planning (MRP), as it is the most important data structure in MRP. Inherent in MRP is the ability to take the finished good and calculate all of the dependent subcomponent need dates. This is called "exploding the BOM." However, not many people get to see how this procedure is actually accomplished, but it's important to be able to visualize it in order to fully understand what occurs when MRP is run. To this end, I have selected a very easy-to-use supply planning application to demonstrate the BOM as it is used by MRP. This software is created by a software vendor called Demand Works and their application is called Smoothie. Smoothie is one of the best environments that I have come across for educating people on how both demand planning and supply planning work in software.

MRP is traditionally performed in the ERP system; however, I want to be sure to point out that Smoothie is not an ERP system. It is an external planning environment that is often connected to ERP systems. Even so, I have selected Smoothie for this demonstration because the BOM in Smoothie is very simple and understandable and because Smoothie has MRP functionality. Using SAP ERP to explain how MRP uses the BOM would be much more difficult and not as clear. If you can understand the BOM as used by Smoothie for MRP, you will understand MRP's interaction with the BOM for any ERP system.

Smoothie contains both demand planning and supply planning functionality, but for this demonstration I will only show tables used in supply planning as the bill of materials is not relevant for demand planning. Demand planning creates forecasts at the finished good or assembly level, and supply planning takes the finished goods forecast and connects that forecast to the subcomponents that make up the finished good. Smoothie's file structure is so simple and well laid out that it is very easy to see how the BOM is exploded depending on a demand.

The MRP BOM

For the purposes of MRP, a BOM is simply a list of input items that connect in a predefined way to an output item, or items, in certain proportions and that takes a certain amount of time to be converted. For discrete manufacturing (things like automobiles, toys and tools), the relationship tends to be between multiple input items and a single output item. However, in process industries, which would include things like chemical or cheese processing, subcomponents can have fractional as well as variable conversion factors that result in a single finished good.

The main requirement of process manufacturing is that the final item cannot be broken down and converted back to the original input products. Therefore, cheese cannot be disassembled into its original components, but an automobile could be disassembled and the parts placed back on a shelf. Process manufacturing industries are also different from discrete manufacturing industries in that one input item can convert to multiple output items, or multiple input items can convert or be combined into a single output item. Another feature of process manufacturing that differs from discrete manufacturing is that the "yield" from one batch to the next can change. This is common in milk products (different concentrations of fat and protein depending upon the batch) as well as the semiconductor chips that come from wafers. With semi-conductor chips, different slides have different numbers of chips with different distinguishing properties. All of these relationship quantities can be easily modeled in a spreadsheet. The spreadsheet or table below (which happens to be the Smoothie BOM input table) demonstrates a process-industry BOM that is exploded by MRP.

from_item	to_item	link_type	offset_days	factor
BEER	ALCOHOL	0	0	0.050
WINE	ALCOHOL	0	0	0.120
LIQUOR	ALCOHOL	0	0	0.400

This is a process BOM because it has a factor, which is less than one, meaning that there is a conversion between quantities and they are expressed as a percentage. The to_item is Alcohol, which is converting to the from_item, which is Beer, Wine, and Liquor. More Alcohol is used in the production of Liquor than Beer, and this is only one of the ingredients to each of these output products. The offset_days is currently set to zero, but in reality, the manufacturing process takes time and should be higher than zero.

Engineering Change Management in SAP ERP

SAP has functionality called Engineering Change Management (ECM), which allows users to apply validity periods to the components that make up the BOM. This functionality is necessary to control how MRP plans future order proposals (planned orders or purchase requisitions) when new components are being phased in and old components are being phased out. Additionally reason codes are used to control how the manufacturing plant changes the BOM. SAP also offers a report that provides visibility into the changed items. However, as I will discuss in Chapter 7: "The BOM Management System: The BMMS," the ECM functionality in SAP ERP is very basic and is built essentially around validity periods. Rather than expecting very much ECM functionality in SAP ERP, it is best to perform engineering change management in the BOM management system, and then reflect the changes in SAP ERP.

Understanding BOM Explosion

BOM explosion is very simple. Prior to the development of computers, BOM explosion was performed manually. MRP automated BOM explosion and calculated the proper purchase order and production order date assignment by working backwards from demand dates. "Explosion" sounds dramatic, but simply refers to the multiplicative calculation performed by the planning system method, in this case MRP. Continuing the previous example, if demand for liquor is 1000 items, then demand for alcohol is 400 units (1000 x 0.4), in addition to a similar multiplication of 1000 for any other items that are connected to the Liquor from_item in the BOM (not shown in the simplified BOM above). Explosion could just as well be called *finished good to input product relationship multiplication,* but that might be a bit too wordy for common usage. The demand for the input products in relation to the BOM is the dependent demand: their demand is "dependent" upon the demand of the finished good. BOM explosion is one of the major value-adds to the MRP procedure. The most important features of MRP are listed in the graphic below:

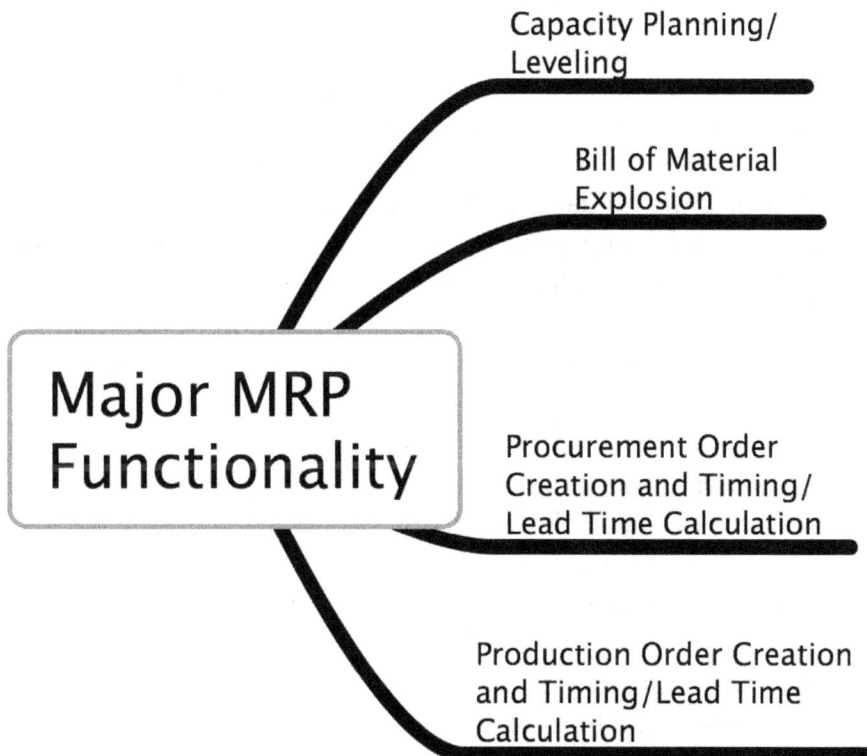

Capacity Planning/
Leveling

Bill of Material
Explosion

Major MRP
Functionality

Procurement Order
Creation and Timing/
Lead Time Calculation

Production Order Creation
and Timing/Lead Time
Calculation

Routings and Work Centers, Companion Master Data Objects to the BOM

As discussed previously, the BOM is connected to two other master data objects. One is the work center, where the work is performed and the other is routings, which is the path production takes through the work centers. Multiple routings are often modeled in the system to account for variations in the manufacturing process. The routing will contain the following information:

1. Make-up of operations, which is the individual steps and how long they take to complete

2. The plant (a routing can be plant-specific or can apply across plants)

3. The work center

4. The setup time, machine time and labor time

5. Operational scrap percentage

In addition to the routing and the BOM, the work centers are connected to the materials that make up the BOM. A work center can be configured to process a single material or multiple materials, and its capacity changes depending upon the material that is processed. The calendars associated with work centers are, of course, different than the factory calendar; the work center calendar will always be smaller or lower in capacity than the factory calendar. A factory must be open in order for a work center to be operational; conversely, just because the factory is open does not mean that the work center is operational. A production line has downtimes for scheduled maintenance and changeovers. This downtime is considered nonproductive time, which is required in order to switch production between different products.

Work centers also have utilization rates, and many applications allow you to set a unique utilization rate for each day. Therefore, a work center with a capacity of 2000 units per hour and a utilization rate of 75 percent for a particular day would have an adjusted capacity of 1500 units per hour.

Multiple activities are performed at a work center. Setup is one example, and machine time is another. Each of the activities at a work center are costed, making the work center both a supply chain modeling object as well as a costing center. Modeling decisions must be made in terms of defining a "resource." For instance, a resource, which is modeled as a single work center, may actually be several machines, but for modeling reasons (and to reduce complexity) the three machines would be one work center. In fact, an entire production line can be modeled as a single work center if the modeler believes it is justified and will meet the business requirements.

This is a resource which is converted from a work center in SAP ERP, but which resides in SAP APO. The resource contains the information that has been described above, including the capacity and the utilization rate. Some applications allow the utilization rate to differ for each day. Work centers and resources process the BOM in both ERP systems and external planning systems and they have implications for both supply planning and production planning as well as production execution and production costing. Work centers are included in supply planning systems so that the supply planning system can incorporate capacity constraints. It is quite common to include production work centers and resources in supply planning systems, but not mandatory.

There are many variations in the manufacturing process and these are reflected in different versions of BOMs, routings and work centers. BOMs for the same finished good can have different quantities of subcomponents depending upon which work centers are used for manufacturing. Variability in the BOM may be caused by work centers that are at different plants but which produce the same finished good. When that is the case, the BOM must be plant-specific (and work centers are always plant-specific). This natural variability is why ERP and external planning systems often assign the slight variations of BOMs, routings and work centers to one another, which leads to the topic of costing BOMs. "Costing BOMs" is a misleading term because the costing is actually assigned at the work centers where the activities are performed. However, the BOM, work centers and routings are so interconnected in ERP and external planning systems that it can make sense to describe alternatives as costing BOMs.

The BOM in External Planning Systems

The MBOM is often discussed as if the ERP system were the only customer for the master data on the supply chain side. However, many companies have moved beyond ERP's basic supply chain functionality for supply chain planning and use external planning systems for both supply and production planning, meaning that there is a secondary update process for the BOM. If a BOM management application is being used, it would be optimal for the BOM management software to first update the ERP system and for the ERP system to update the planning system. As has been discussed, the BOM attenuates when it is transferred from the EBOM to the MBOM. The external planning system also uses what is technically an MBOM as does the ERP system; however, there is a further attenuation and removal of fields between the ERP system and the external planning system, as the external planning system uses the MBOM in a much more limited way than even the ERP system.

The example below shows how the BOM appears in a best-of-breed production planning and scheduling application from PlanetTogether.

PlanetTogether has a flexible and relatively easy-to-understand and easy-to-change BOM. It should also be noted that PlanetTogether is a production planning and scheduling application, which is different from a supply planning application such as Smoothie, which was shown earlier in the chapter. This should serve to highlight the fact that the BOM is used by multiple systems on the supply chain side. A BOM may be represented in a company's ERP system and in the supply planning system, as well as the production planning system. The ERP system typically serves as the "hub" for BOM information in the supply chain area. This does not always have to be the case. As all of the external planning systems eventually send back recommendations to the ERP system to execute, it makes sense to have all the systems in synch. However, the one disadvantage of this is that many planning systems have better BOM interfaces than ERP systems.

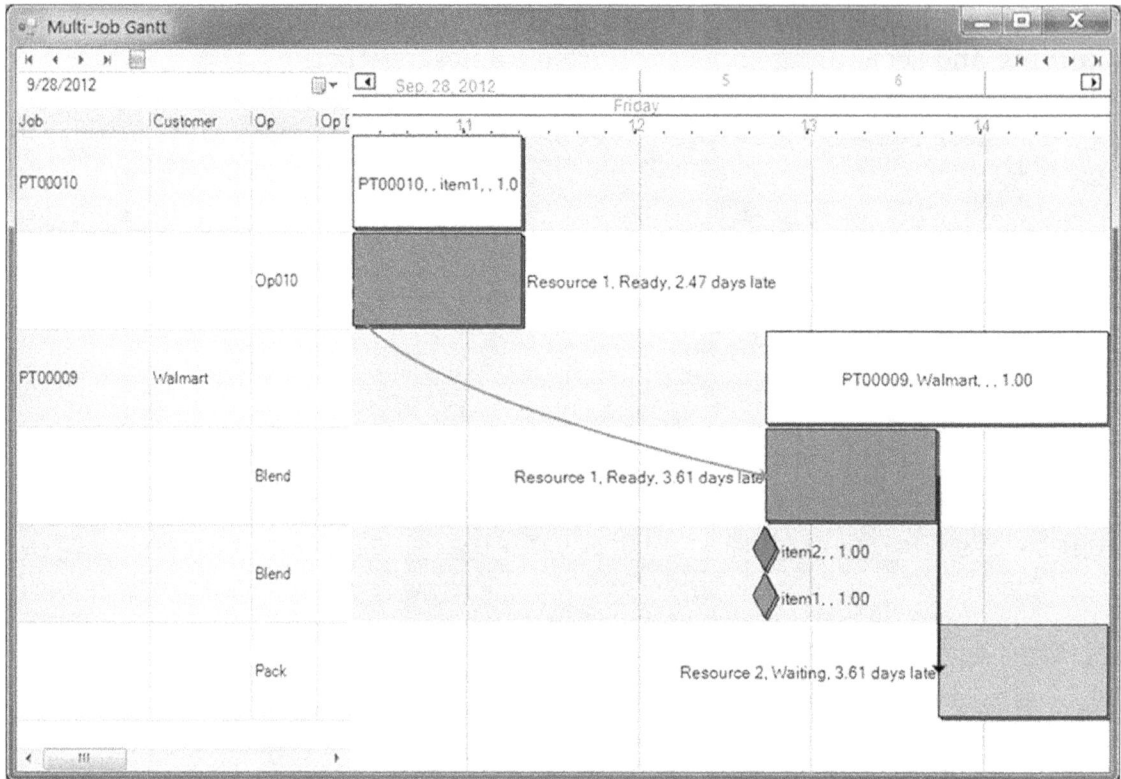

This screenshot shows a close up of the colorized relationship of the BOM as it displays in PlanetTogether's scheduling interface.

The Process Flow of the BOM in Supply Chain Systems

Planning takes place in the demand planning system at the assembly level (and takes place without the BOM). After the demand plan is complete, it is sent to supply planning. Exploding the BOM is part of the supply planning process, where the assemblies, final assemblies or finished goods (depending upon your preferred terminology) for which there is a demand are multiplied by the dependent products (subassemblies and raw materials, etc.) and the items within the BOM. Therefore if 100 units of the finished good A is demanded in August, and the BOM states that there are 2 units of the subassembly B required, which in turn requires 3 units of the component C, the total demand is:

1. 100 units of A

2. 200 units of B

3. 600 units of C

If the lead times for B and C from the example above are one month and two months respectively, then to meet demand for A in August, planned production or purchase orders for B would be created in June, and for C would be created in April.

MRP's ability to adjust thousands or hundreds of thousands of finished good orders and for all dependent demand was a great benefit for supply and production planning (that is until they found out that the efforts of the BOM software were undermined by poor master data accuracy). For several decades, a major consulting and software area in the developed countries was the conversion of companies to MRP-based systems. In fact, forty years after MRP started to be adopted by industry, most companies still use a combination of MRP and DRP (which itself is based upon MRP) to perform supply and production planning.

Where the BOM explosion is performed is a decision point for projects with external planning systems. For instance, materials can be planned only at the finished good level in the planning system and then the BOM can be exploded in the ERP system. Alternatively, the BOM can be exploded in the external planning system and planning production orders for finished goods, subassemblies and components. This increases the data flow between the systems; however, increasingly I am observing that companies want to have their planners use one system primarily, instead of planning finished goods in the planning systems and all other dependent demand items in the ERP system.

http://www.scmfocus.com/sapplanning/2012/07/18/where-material-and-procurement-planning-occurs-in-sap-erp-and-apo/

How Is BOM Management Software Different?
While the planning system should have an easily alterable representation of the BOM, it's important to not confuse the BOM representation function in ERP systems and planning systems with a full BOM management solution. Supply chain systems show the BOM in a limited way, but also tend to have only one view.

By the end of this book, it will be entirely obvious how different the BOM in supply chain systems is from the BOM in BMMS, but generally this is a tremendous blind spot for both executives and managers who work in supply chain systems. The information that will follow is well-known by BMMS vendors, but for whatever reason has not been broadly disseminated. BOM management software is specifically designed around a set of requirements that is greater than representing the BOM for a planning or ERP system, including the connection of CAD CAM drawings to the BOM and sophisticated change management and collaboration capabilities. Supply chain professionals touch the BOM in only one way, and often miss the other applications of the BOM throughout the company. This limited viewpoint often leads to a very common mistake: attempting to stretch the limited ability of supply planning systems and ERP systems so that they perform full BOM management. BOM management is much bigger than just supply chain planning and execution, and requires specialized software for which there are some very good vendors. However, because the only exposure many people have to BOM management is the limited functionality in ERP systems, these professionals do not understand what a fully-capable BOM management solution even looks like or how they work. So that you can understand the actual capability of the software category, I recommend logging into the online trial of Arena Solutions. If you spend time understanding Arena, you will very quickly understand what "real" BOM management is.

Conclusion

Supply chain planning can be performed with either ERP systems at a relatively simple level, or with ERP and external planning systems at a much more complex level. However, both systems use the same BOM, with the external planning system having its BOM information populated as part of the normal integration data transfer process.

The MBOM is based upon a subset of the EBOM. The EBOM comes into existence well before the MBOM, and it's only necessary to create the MBOM once the product nears production and subcomponents and parts must be procured in anticipation of manufacturing. Some things in the BMMS, such as lead times, are not included in the MBOM in the ERP or planning system, but instead are stored in the individual product records. Therefore, moving information from a

BMMS means splitting data into multiple ERP and planning system master data objects. MBOMs are extremely simple when compared to EBOMs, as typically they only include the bare necessities required to enable the manufacturing of a product. Furthermore, ERP vendors spend little development effort on their BOM functionality beyond supporting planning, which is another reason as to why they are a poor choice of systems to maintain the BOM (in addition to the BOM being incompletely represented in ERP). Some ERP documentation may seem to contradict this fact; however, a detailed analysis of the BOM functionality in SAP ERP (and specifically the BOM usage categories such as design, costing, production, sales and distribution, spare part, etc.) make it clear that creating a design/engineering BOM in SAP ERP does not provide very much value to the company, particularly because design and engineering do not use SAP ERP or other ERP systems. The functionality offered by ERP systems is not directed toward design and engineering and design and engineering resources use other systems. As is described in Chapter 7: "The BOM Management System: The BMMS," the design solution I recommend throughout this book is to keep the EBOM in a BMMS, manage the complexity of the BOM and make changes to the BOMs in the BMMS, and then port the BOM data to the ERP system, rather than maintaining the design and engineering BOMs in the ERP system. The ERP system is used to manage the simpler BOM requirements, which is more appropriate for the limited BOM functionality provided by ERP systems. This simple change in how a company manages its BOM information can significantly improve the company's capabilities. For instance, this design removes the need to use phantom assemblies in the ERP system, as BOMs that are irrelevant for planning are not set up in the ERP system. Productivity benefits because ERP systems do not have to "stretch" to meet business requirements that they are not designed to meet. This is actually an important issue related to all software: companies will often add a great deal of functionality, but some of the functionality is inappropriate for the need and is better performed in other software. Because of the competing interest between vendors, the bias of many decision-making groups within the company, and the under funding of solution architecture roles (the fact that is it is generally much easier to obtain funding for a specific application resource than for a solution architect to fit the pieces together), many of these decisions regarding the best application to perform different functions are poorly made.

The fact that ERP systems are not good systems of record for the BOM is all true and undeniable for those familiar with BOM management options. However, I continually find myself reading self-confident statements in requirements documents on supply chain software implementation projects that are similar to the following:

> *Maintenance of data will happen in the ERP system as much as possible.*

This would be tantamount to reading:

> *When traveling between countries, all employees should ride bicycles to reach their destination.*

Both statements are definitive, yet quite wrong and quite prescriptive in proposing the worst way to do something. The second statement is only viewed as more ludicrous that the first because of one's exposure level to the alternatives. The reason I say this is that the exact approach outlined in the first statement has been attempted at thousands of ERP implementations, never with good outcomes. ERP vendors that promise to bring "best practices" in all areas to their clients recommend this approach. Can anyone really say with a straight face that maintaining BOM data in ERP systems is a best practice? The fields that are available within SAP ERP were listed in this chapter in order to provide a general feel for how limited the MBOM is within ERP systems. A constant problem with the term "best practices" is that it is often translated loosely into "whatever the software vendor has to offer."

Exposure to the BOM user interface in SAP ERP should convince any person that maintaining and making changes to the BOM in SAP ERP is a poor practice. SAP makes the BOM difficult to understand and difficult to update. The interface was designed to enter information so it may be used by the system; it is not designed to actually interact with the information. Furthermore, SAP ERP has weak search and associative querying capabilities with respect to BOM data. In order to give a comparison, screenshots were provided of the search and associative capability within Arena Solutions. All of these issues generalize to other ERP systems, although many systems may have slightly better BOM interfaces than SAP ERP.

While MRP is normally run in ERP systems, with more advanced supply and production planning methods applied in external planning systems, the limited BOM visibility in SAP ERP and ERP systems in general prompted me to use Demand Works Smoothie to explain how the BOM is used by MRP. The example in this chapter demonstrated that the multiplicative relationship between the finished product and the subcomponents make up the heart of MRP. The MRP procedure is run for every combination of product and location, and production orders and purchase orders are assigned to a product location. The MRP orders are then run through controlling parameters, which tend to increase the ordering amount (both for procurement and production) in order to create more economically efficient batches. In this chapter, the MRP example demonstrated that BOMs change depending upon whether they are for discrete manufacturing (e.g., pens, toys, books) or process manufacturing (e.g., paint, chemicals, cheese).

BOM explosion is performed in the ERP system, and sometimes in the external planning system. BOM explosion can be part of MRP, but can also be performed without MRP. Explosion is the process of taking the number of finished goods forecasted or demanded (depending upon whether the process is "build to stock" or "build to order") in a future period and multiplying—or exploding—it by the number of subcomponents. BOM explosion is one of the major value-adds to the MRP procedure. It enables a company to know the quantities of different products and—combined with lead-time estimates—when these quantities must be available in the factory to support production.

There is little difference in the logic of how a BOM is presented and used in an ERP system and in a planning system. More advanced supply chain planning methods, such as cost optimization, process the product location combinations in different sequences, but when it comes to the BOM there is a great deal of similarity across the supply planning methods with respect to how the BOM is processed. The main difference arises not with the method of supply planning used, but with what level of the BOM hierarchy is processed.

BOM management software is designed to meet all of a company's BOM requirements, including the following:

1. The ability to represent the complete BOM, all of its fields and all of its associated files (CAD, PDF)

2. The ability to both search and find associations within the BOM and even across BOMs

3. The ability to be accessed by users inside and outside of the company

4. A highly-capable authorization model that allows each user to only change specific BOMs and portions of BOMs

5. The ability to hold the many versions of a BOM, including its initial development and the changes after its initial development

6. The ability to leverage information within the BMMS to improve supplier management, subcomponent pricing, and contract manufacturer pricing

The above is only a partial list, but it should be sufficient to explain how the design of a BMMS system differs from an ERP or external planning system. The BOM functionality of ERP and external planning systems is only enough to perform manufacturing and procurement planning. Hopefully, this chapter has explained how different these requirements are from one another. With this background knowledge, it is appropriate to discuss the BMMS, which is the topic of the next chapter.

CHAPTER 7

The BOM Management System: The BMMS

Understanding the BMMS

A BMMS can be explained and understood from many perspectives. However, one perspective that is often not explained is that the BMMS creates a central repository of the BOM and all related information in a consistent form and in a single system. This is only possible because any authorized individual, either inside or outside of the company that "owns" the BMMS can access or alter the data (consistent with their authorization level). The ability of a BMMS to allow this collaboration adds tremendous value and keeps the various companies working off of the same information, something that has been a constant problem with BOM management since BOM maintenance began. However, it is very important that the BMMS system be extremely user friendly, because if it is not, then individuals and companies will not be inclined to use the BMMS system, and instead choose to export the data to their own computers and manipulate it there. Any changes made on individual computers rather than within the BMMS means that the BMMS data does not reflect those changes.

Once a company has implemented a BMMS, those that work with the system can experience great efficiencies, as pointed out by Antti Saaksvori and Anselmi Immonen:

> *Kenneth McIntosh has proposed that in companies operating in the field of manufacturing industry, the planning engineers expend 15–40 percent of their working hours doing routine searches of information and retrieving routine information from separate systems.*

Therefore, those who work with the BMMS not only save time looking for the required information, but also avoid spending time to ensure they actually have the up-to-date version of the item. Furthermore, I do not think that McIntosh's estimate includes the time that planning engineers spend asking engineers in other companies if they have made any changes to an item that they plan to work on.

Multi-dimensional Relationships

One easy way of understanding the highly linked nature of a BOM and its sub-components is to consider that one subcomponent is often part of more than one parent component. By using a relational BOM configuration, which is different from a relational database; you can use a relational database, but follow a restricted hierarchical model in your BOM configuration. When the subcomponent is changed in one location, it immediately affects all parent components; immediacy in that change and how it affects other BOMs is the desired end state. The goal is for all parent products (i.e., BOMs) to be updated instantly when a subcomponent is changed, regardless of the product's life-stage. The updated part data is then sent over to the planning system, where a flag is changed to tell the planning system that the part should no longer be planned. Updating this data is as important as the algorithms you use to produce a forecast.

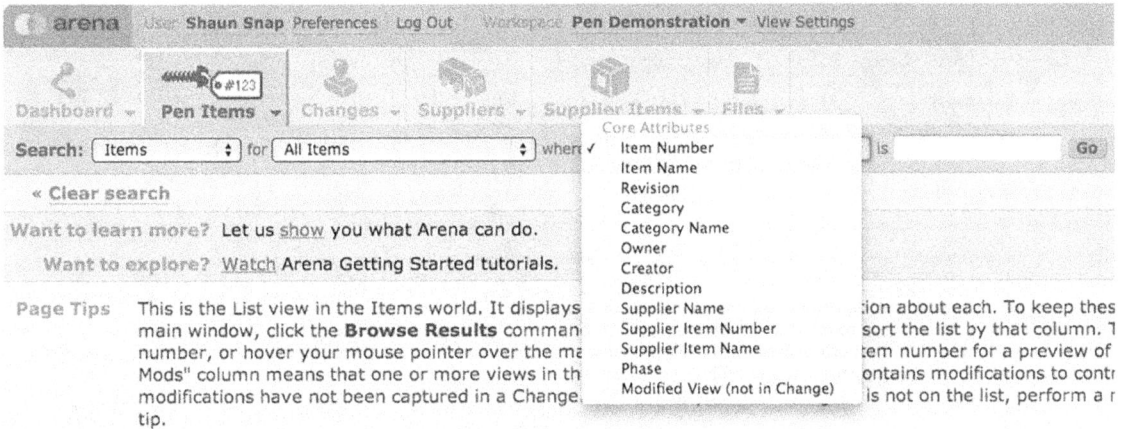

In Arena, BOM, parts, suppliers, etc. can be easily searched and are easily interrelated.

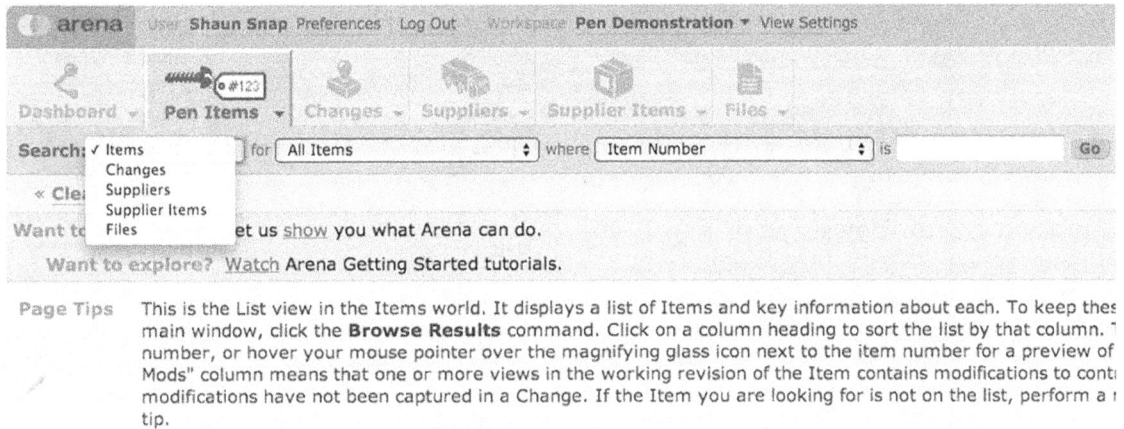

We can select the item...

arena   User: **Shaun Snap** Preferences / Log Out   Workspace: **SCM Focus EveryRoad GPS Trial** ▾ Edit Settings   Show Print View Hide Page Tips Help ?

Dashboard ▾   Arena Trial Items ▾   Requests ▾   Changes ▾   Suppliers ▾   Supplier Items ▾   Files ▾   Reports ▾

Search: [Items ⇕] for [All Items ⇕] where [Item Number ⇕] is [EveryRoadGPS] Go

New Item **Import Items**

Need help? Find application shortcuts, tips and on-demand tutorials in the Arena Trial Center.

Ready for more? Learn how to get started with Arena in less than 5 days for as little as $99/user per month.

Page Tips This is the List view in the Items world. It displays a list of Items and key information about each. To keep these list results open while browsing them in the main window, click the **Browse Results** command. Click on a column heading to sort the list by that column. To learn more about an Item, click its item number, or hover your mouse pointer over the magnifying glass icon next to the item number for a preview of the Specs view of the Item. An icon in the "Wkg Mods" column means that one or more views in the working revision of the Item contains modifications to controlled data – the icon is orange if those modifications have not been captured in a Change. If the Item you are looking for is not on the list, perform a new search using the search dialog above this tip.

List of
All Arena Trial Items

✧ Browse Results

94 Items found | Show All   ☐ Search within these results   **Export Found Items**

Items 1 - 20 « Previous Next »

#	☐	🛠	⚙	⚙	Item Number	Item Name	Category	Files	Rqmts	Phase	Prototype Cost	Production Cost	Wkg Mods
01	☐		⚙ ▾		20-0001 rev B 🔍	EveryRoad GPS, Shippable, US Model 300	Finished Good	📄2 ▾		In Prod	$305.47413	$156.28227	
02	☐		⚙ ▾		20-0002 rev B 🔍	EveryRoad GPS Car Navigation Unit - Model 300	Product Assembly	📄2 ▾	📄 ? ▾	In Prod	$240.10046	$132.7286	
03	☐		⚙ ▾		20-0003 rev A 🔍	EveryRoad, Front Bezel Assembly	Subassembly	📄2 ▾	📄 ✓ ▾	In Prod	$14.26	$6.99	⚠ ▾
04	☐		⚙ ▾		20-0004 rev B 🔍	EveryRoad, Rear Assembly	Subassembly	📄2 ▾	📄 ✗ ▾	In Prod	$225.21686	$125.2738	
05	☐		⚙ ▾		20-0005 rev A 🔍	Package Documentation	Subassembly	📄		In Prod	$2.98	$1.08	⚠ ▾
06	☐		⚙ ▾		20-0015 rev B 🔍	EveryRoad, PCBA, Model 300	Printed Circuit Board Assembly	📄6 ▾	📄 ✗ ▾	In Prod	$215.47726	$122.631	

⌐ **Show Only**   **Keep**   **Save to Dashboard**   **Add to BOM**   **Add to Change**   **Add to Request**   **Assign to Category**

...or we can search by supplier.

The search by supplier very quickly leads to the parts supplied by the supplier. In Arena, it is never difficult to get to related objects.

While a BOM is a complete representation of a final product, it is made up of a hierarchy of parts that are all inter-related (or should I say, that is one way of interpreting or showing the BOM).

Notice the indented BOM above. Many people who consult in BOMs often discuss flattening the BOM. Purchasing often wants to see a list of items rather than the hierarchical relationship. However, if a system can represent a BOM as either flat or indented, there is no reason to have to choose only one way of managing the BOM.

Here the BOM is flat and ready to be used by the purchasing department or other groups that prefer to see the BOM this way. Flattening the BOMs was a major point of contention among BOM experts; however, it is completely mitigated with the correct technology. I have included the following quotations to show how much emphasis has been placed on flattening BOMs in the past.

Statement: *Even well structured bills have crumpled under the weight of constant maintenance. The more bills there are scattered throughout the company, the harder it is to maintain them accurately. Engineering is working on Revision Z, while the plant floor is still working from Revision B. Costs are being figured on Revision C, and no one in the company can figure out why the product isn't getting produced but is costing more than expected. A single master bill of material is much easier to maintain.* — Bills of Material, For a Lean Enterprise

My Response: Arena has no problem with an enormous amount of nesting, and encourages nesting as it allows the company to access more of Arena's functionality. Arena also uses nesting as an organizing principle of the BOM. Many of the benefits of nesting are described elsewhere in this book. The revisions made by engineering and the plant floor as discussed in the above quote would not exist with a BMMS. The different revisions would simply exist in the BMMS. When a product is ready to be copied for a different system, the copy is made and the subset BOM of the system-of-record BOM in the BMMS is then replicated to the non-BMMS systems.

Statement: Now, instead of forecasting instruments, we can use planning bills to forecast part requirements and build the instrument to customer order. In some cases, it may be impossible for you to get down to a single level bill of material for an entire product. The important point is that the bill mirrors the process, not the other way around. — Bills of Material, For a Lean Enterprise

My Response: Not with a BMMS. A BMMS allows for unlimited nesting, and typically has no problem modeling any BOM. There is no reason to flatten the BOM (to remove the hierarchy) because the hierarchy is an actual functionality of the BOM in the BMMS.

Statement: There are many reasons—some legitimate, some not— for levels in the bill. Additional levels in the bill of material may be added to document what is happening in the manufacturing process, such as the creation of sub-assemblies or intermediaries that will be inventoried. In too many cases, levels in the bill were used as a substitute for operational steps best identified in the routing—when a product went to a different work station, it was assigned a different number. — Bills of Material, For a Lean Enterprise

My Response: With a BMMS, there is no reason to try to limit the indentedness, hierarchy or levels of the BOM.

Statement: The number of levels in the bill should be minimized. Each level in the bill creates extra paperwork, extends the lead-time and increases the work necessary to maintain the bill. In dealing with bills, we say that shallower is

better. A bill that has the fewest possible levels is easier to maintain and results in less paperwork. Too often we include levels in the bill for such reasons as labor collection or WIP inventory value or to gather work at a particular workstation, functions that are better served by using the routing. The only legitimate reason for a level in the bill of material is planning and scheduling. — Bills of Material, For a Lean Enterprise

My Response: This statement may be true without a BMMS, but is not true if one has a BMMS. Arena can manage any number of levels in the BOM, and these levels actually provide the BMMS BOM with greater flexibility and more functionality. In fact, some of Arena's functionality is based upon intensive nesting. However, I agree that the routing should never be in the BOM. But it is not true that planning and scheduling is the only legitimate reason for a level in the bill of material. There are many reasons, and in fact, the BOM is most effective as a hierarchical object.

Statement: *Simple, organized Bills of Material (BOM) are not difficult to create or maintain. It is a tedious and sometimes complicated endeavor, however. The interdependency of components and their product structures can create a nightmare in maintenance. A worse nightmare occurs when they are not maintained. Again, this is not difficult, just tedious. A methodical eye for detail is required, with a strong steadfast process for change control.* — *Supply Chain Brutalization*

My Response: This is only true if you do not use a BMMS. A BMMS manages most of these things for the user.

However, the cost and degree of complexity of each part can span any part of the continuum. Some parts are simple commodities that do not change very frequently, while others are just the opposite. It may be that a majority of the activity, and revisions on all of the parts on the BOM are on a small minority of the parts. It may also be that the costs are driven by just a few of the parts.

A system for estimating production costs must use a data model powerful enough to capture the complexities of real world cost data. Much of this complexity arises from the fact that real products are a combination of commodity components, custom components and a variety of manufacturing processes, each with its own cost structure and considerations. For example, commodity components and processes are typically purchased from multiple sources, some of which may be distributors and some of which may be manufacturers. To correctly handle this common situation, a tool for capturing product cost data must have a data model that comprehends the supply chain, and the manufacturers, distributors, and the process vendors that it comprises. — "The Arena Solutions Guide to Outsourcing: Removing Barriers, Maintaining Boundaries," Arena Solutions, 2011

My Response: The components subportions of the BOM are their own objects. The ability to access and update these objects can be controlled, so, for example, a supplier or design consultancy can access and work on just one component of a BOM, even though there are hundreds or thousands of parts. Likewise, one supplier or design consultancy may interact with hundreds of parts, which are scattered across any number of BOMs; they are assigned a subset of the overall parts database with which they may interact.

Essentially, it is up to the administrator of the BMMS solution as to which BOMs, and even what portion of the BOMs, each user can access; each participant can only see and manipulate a subset of the overall BOM database. Each part has an approved list of parties that can see and interact with it. This list is set up when the BOM is first created in the BMMS system.

Imagine one thousand external parties (of all types) logging into the BMMS and continually interacting with and changing different parts in the BOM, each user oblivious to the rest of the parts database or to the segments of the BOM that they cannot access. Of course, this type of access means updating the user privileges, but this is a straightforward task. In many cases, deciding who should have access to the BOM would not fall to a single administrator, but would be a task that is shared by multiple individuals with the domain expertise on different products. Therefore, the administration function does not need to be a centralized role.

Structured Communication Capabilities Provided by the BMMS

Everything I have described up to this point has been related to instantly updating parts and keeping the BOM database consistent, controlled and sound. However,

BMMS vendors have also figured out how to leverage all of this dynamic collaboration into radically improved communication. If we think about it, once all of the parts have been assigned to all of the different types of users (both internal and external), communication between users can be accomplished through the BMMS. Using the BMMS to communicate has some of the same implications of social media, although I don't propose that the users tell personal stories or post pictures of their vacations to Venezuela. However, the underlying design is quite similar to social media in that participants can access updates in a universal and instantaneous fashion and communication is routed to only the relevant participants based upon an assignment to some differentiating object. Of all the collaborative applications that I have analyzed, the two that set the standard are social media websites (for consumers) and BMMS systems (for the enterprise market). Other categories of applications (such as collaborative supply chain planning applications) don't even come close to the capabilities provided by social media and BMMS systems.

Modern corporate communication is defined by email. Before social networking software, emails were the primary method of computerized social interaction between individuals. However, with social media, communication to groupings of people in a controlled fashion was made possible. The possibilities for communicating with a community have been a major reason for social media's rise and overwhelming influence over the Internet. Social media is essentially a new communications medium as is evidenced by the fact that it was adopted first by young people. However, as social media sites have grown in popularity, the average age of their users has also increased, indicating that this form of group communication is a significant improvement over other types of communication.

And what are these improvements? On Facebook, when a person has something to post, those on the approved friend list can all see the posting, and if someone chooses to respond, then the rest of those in the group can also see the response. None of this requires any email addresses to be typed in or decisions to be made as to whom to include on the distribution list. Of course you have to decide which information you want certain people to see (i.e., you can create a "close acquaintance" list or a business list or any number of lists or subsets of your friends list). You also have to decide if you only want your friends to see something, or the friends of your friends to see something. If you operate a page that people "like" then it's much simpler of course. I guess you allude to this in the sentence, "All of this is managed through grouping."

In fact, the person responding is not required to know all, or any, of the people in the social network of the person to whom they are responding. All of this is managed through groupings of people who are authorized to view certain messages. As a result, communication on the Internet has changed greatly to automated control over message distribution. Furthermore, many-to-many communication now requires little effort on the part of the participants.

When people comment on articles and blogs, they are essentially engaging in the same type of activity. By commenting on a blog or article or otherwise actively declaring an interest in the blog, one is thereby assigned to it and can opt to have any future comments or update notifications forwarded to their email account.

When this concept is applied to the BMMS, one can see the many benefits. One benefit has been mentioned: convenience and the low effort level required to keep up on part status. A second benefit is that one-on-one conversations occur less frequently, which means that people are not left out of the communications where they have a need and a right to know about the details discussed. The BMMS does not stop people from picking up the telephone and conversing on topics, or sending an email outside the BMMS, and not every topic of conversation needs to necessarily be in the BMMS message archive. But the BMMS naturally redirects communication away from one-on-one communication because it is so simple and natural to use. Arena Solutions uses the terminology of "structured communication" to describe this feature of an effective BMMS.

> *The current practice of collaborating within product development groups is unstructured communication. Information is broadcasted one-to-one: engineers talk to each other, the project manager talks to the purchasing agent, and so on.*
> — "Collaborative Tools for Product Development: A New Approach,"
> Arena Solutions, 2011

This structuring of communication is extremely important because more and more we are seeing that collaborators on BOMs are located in different companies and, in many instances, may even be in different countries. A person sitting at the OEM (Original Equipment Manufacturer) in San Jose may have never been introduced to manufacturing engineers sitting in Taiwan, and may not even know the names of the people assigned to that team. However, as soon as the right individuals are added to the part, everyone's messages are available to read.

Another outcome of this type of automated communication is that it integrates the individuals that are part of the system. That is, users are notified via messages when certain changes have been made, prompting them to go through and complete natural follow-on tasks. It's important that users receive this notification because completion of the previous task was required before beginning the next. A person who is assigned to a part can quickly ascertain the status of the item simply by reviewing the BMMS. With a BMMS, there are fewer opportunities for miscommunication and for things to fall between the cracks.

How Are Associations Created in a BMMS?

On social networks such as Facebook, individuals are connected to other individuals, thus creating a group. The most elemental master data object in most social media is the individual. Tom, Peter, and Mary are all connected to one another; however, Tom is connected to people with whom Peter and Mary are not and vice versa.

For a BMMS, the main master data object is actually a part (not the BOM because individuals are not assigned to the overall BOM, as has been discussed already up to this point). Individuals are then assigned to a part, and become members of a group who are all satellites of that part. James who works in Engineering within the OEM in San Jose, and Li who works in Taiwan, may both share assignment to fifty parts, but for Li these may be the only parts he is assigned to. James may be assigned to hundreds of parts. Li and James can see all communication for the fifty-shared parts, and of course send messages that are seen by the group. They are also alerted when new messages have been created for that part. These messages can be forwarded to their company email, so that they know when there are occurrences with their parts. They may use the message to gain perspective, or alternatively, they may choose to log in to the BMMS to review the message, change, etc. which led to the message's origin. Arena Solutions elaborates on this idea:

> *Each user can be assigned an access role that provides the appropriate visibility and change privileges without giving unrestricted access to intellectual property. Sensitive information such as cost quotes can be hidden from particular groups of users if desired. Component manufacturers can be restricted to particular components or assemblies that they supply.*
>
> — "Collaborative Tools for Product Development: A New Approach,"
> Arena Solutions, 2011

What was previously considered an impossible goal is now possible, as described in the quote from Arena Solutions below:

> *Throughout the lifecycle of a product, numerous revisions of BOMs are created and communicated to multiple internal and external teams. Keeping everyone on the same latest revision of a BOM spreadsheet is an impossible feat.*
>
> — "Manufacturing Outsourcing: Seven Common Pitfalls to Avoid,"
> Bijan Dastmalchi, Richard Vermeij, Arena Solutions, 2007

Details for
SCM Focus EveryRoad GPS Trial

Summary ▾ | Access ▾ | Integrations | Items ▾ | Requests ▾ | Changes ▾ | Reports ▾ | Attributes ▾ | Categories ▾ | Requirements ▾ | Lists | **Recent Activity**

Access   Exports   Report Runs   Show: User Access ⬍ Go

5 recent logins found. All recent logins shown |

#	Login Time	Name	Role Type	Role Name	Duration	Connected Through	Originating IP	Domain
01	Saturday, Jan 7, 2012 09:46	Shaun Snap	Employee	Full Employee [Production Revision Creation]	Logged In	Arena	108.161.20.6	unknown
02	Friday, Jan 6, 2012 19:17	Shaun Snap	Employee	Full Employee [Production Revision Creation]	8 m	Arena	108.161.20.6	unknown
03	Friday, Jan 6, 2012 15:30	Shaun Snap	Employee	Full Employee [Production Revision Creation]	7 m	Arena	108.161.20.6	unknown
04	Friday, Jan 6, 2012 09:58	Shaun Snap	Employee	Full Employee [Production Revision Creation]	0 m	Arena	206.169.7.132	206-169-7-132.arenasolutions.com
05	Friday, Jan 6, 2012 09:54	Arena Technical Support	Partner	Full Partner [No Revision Creation]	3 m	Arena	206.169.7.132	206-169-7-132.arenasolutions.com

On the Arena Full Detail view shown above, one can also see who is logged in and when.

While the messages are made available through a secondary copy that resides in the user's email inbox, the "system of record" for these messages is actually the BMMS. This provides archival capability, so that at any time the messages can be reviewed. A manager who oversees hundreds of parts, each of which may be in various stages of the design process, may not focus intensively on any of the parts. However, when an issue arises or when he wants to know a part's status, he can easily find out not only where the part is, but can also read all the messages that have led to the current state. With emails forwarded by the BMMS to his company account, a manager can monitor many more parts than any other conceivable type of BOM management design. This type of monitoring would not be possible using a spreadsheet, where the manager would have to "scan" lists of information in a spreadsheet format to find the changes that have occurred. Instead, messages on different parts arrive on specific topics whenever a new message is created, which greatly increase the manager's productivity level.

The Benefits to Commercial Terms and Negotiation

Up to this point, I have primarily described the benefits brought to the communication process by the BMMS in terms of reduced effort and improved social media-type interaction. Benefits also extend to the contracting company and the subcontractor, through better accuracy and visibility during the commercial and negotiating aspects of the procurement process. The relationship between a buyer and a vendor can be confrontational, and unfortunately too many companies take this confrontational track. The buyer wants to get the lowest price and the vendor the highest. But partnerships can also be approached from the perspective of mutual benefit.

The risk associated with any contract is an important factor in contract negotiations. Vendors who are uncertain what their costs will be have a tendency to quote their price higher. Accurate costing is the main benefit with respect to improving contract negotiations between companies. This is a hugely overlooked benefit to BMMS software.

> *Some CMs are hesitant to provide an accurate breakdown of cost to a detailed level that specifies material cost, cost of acquisition (or material mark-up), labor, test, manufacturing overhead, and profit or gross*

margin. But without clear visibility to the cost breakdown, how can you know what assumptions were used in quoting your product, or what cost improvement opportunities there may be in the future? How will new products be priced in the future? Is the CM giving you a price they can sustain, or are they "buying" your business initially and expecting to raise prices when they have your business?

Unless you have had the early discussions up front on what your supply chain model will look like, your CM quote can increase or decrease substantially. As an example, what "inventory turns" were assumed during the quoting process?

— "Manufacturing Outsourcing: Seven Common Pitfalls to Avoid,"
Bijan Dastmalchi, Richard Vermeij, Arena Solutions, 2007

A BMMS will not magically align the institutional incentives of the buyer and the seller, but it will provide more clarity to each party and reduce the risk because the product that is to be procured is more of a known quantity to each party. A well-implemented BMMS can also reduce the administration required to keep up with changes to the BOM, which itself lowers costs.

All suppliers know that some customers are much more expensive to service than others due to demands for higher service levels or higher quality control, which is essentially a different grade or standard. How difficult a company is to work with can also affect a supplier's costs, including things like how long it takes the company to get back on correspondence, how many changes are made to the part, how late in the process the changes are made, how complete the specifications are and other design information that is shared with the supplier or contract manufacturer.

Over time, suppliers tend to develop a gauge of how difficult and expensive each buyer will be, and to approximate and bid higher prices (if they can) for the more difficult buyers. Of course, some buyers who are difficult to deal with are so large and represent such a significant amount of business that the supplier has few options. However, not every company is so large that it can afford to interact with its suppliers the way that Walmart and General Motors have become notorious for, without expecting to pay a price premium. A company can be considered "difficult to work with" for any number of reasons, ranging from its financial terms and willingness to pay on time, to the level of internal bureaucracy, to how many changes they request on short notice.

A buyer can also be more difficult to work with if it lacks an effective BMMS. As a natural outcome of not having a BMMS, their BOM information will be disorganized. They are less able to provide the quality, clarity and consistency of information required for the supplier to get the information they need. The implication is that a quality BMMS system can make a company more desirable to suppliers, resulting in better prices and better terms. This is described very effectively by Arena Solutions:

> *During the bidding process with a contract manufacturer, an OEM's design can change, and the OEM needs to be certain that the contract manufacturer is aware of the changes when they occur. Traditionally, this means a lot of phone calls, faxes and emails, followed by double-checking the contract manufacturer's bid to make sure it's accurate. With Arena, the OEM can subscribe the contract manufacturer to the part or the assembly in question. Whenever a change is released, the contract manufacturer is notified and a record of that notification is preserved. If multiple contract manufacturers are involved, each one is automatically working with the updated data. The OEM does not need to worry about whether the contract manufacturer has the adequate IT structure to incorporate the change into its data set—the data remains centralized in Arena and instantly available.*
> —"Whose BOM is it Anyway? A Product Disaster Story: 3 Tips for Taking Control of Your Bill Of Materials," Arena Solutions, 2011

Think about the above quotation for a minute, and imagine you are a supplier or contract manufacturer. Which type of company, given that the volume and price is the same, would you prefer to deal with: the one with the BMMS or the one without?

The possibilities for improved efficiency in the bidding process are quite dramatic. The BMMS improves this process through:

    a. Improvement over changes and revisions to the BOM
    b. Communication of the product documentation
    c. The enhanced control and security of the integrated solution

On the flip-side, the OEM also receives a better picture regarding their risk, as any bidding change can be immediately reflected in the overall cost of the BOM, thus improving feedback about costs all along the product development timeline. Costs can begin with the OEM's own internal estimations, which are gradually overwritten with the quotations from the suppliers. If the overall combined price of all the BOM seems to be far enough off of the original estimates, the OEM can make adjustments to the product specification to either increase or decrease the price. By making the changes as early as possible, partners do not have to invest time in repeatedly revising cost estimates. Alternatively, if what a supplier makes is simply not a good fit for that particular product, the supplier can exit the quotation process gracefully and not waste their time. This overall benefit is described in the quotation from Arena Solutions below:

> *Web-native, BOM-centric solutions also substantially improve aggregation of product data: a well-designed BOM data model can easily incorporate specifications, sourcing, and pricing data, and each member of the product team can be assigned specific areas of responsibility for certain types of data and certain levels of the BOM. Because data is captured within a BOM structure, aggregation of costs data can be handled automatically—when a new component cost is entered, the whole product cost estimates are immediately and automatically updated to reflect the new information.*
> — "Collaborative Tools for Product Development: A New Approach,"
> Arena Solutions, 2011

Most companies use BOM management solutions that simply lack the sophistication necessary to support a full analysis of costing. Costing can change for many reasons, and the assumptions of product grade, lead-time expectations, quantities ordered and many other factors can all affect the price. These price changes can be quite significant and easily make the enormous differences in the eventual profit level of the product, as described in the quote from Arena Solutions below:

> *In addition to the large cost differences for prototypes of custom components, there are often significant cost differences between prototype and production prices for commodity components. During development, commodity parts are purchased in small quantities on short lead times to enable rapid prototyping. Vendors that specialize in servicing this market charge substantially higher prices for providing small quantities of parts quickly—generally two to five times the price of the same components in volume. In order to avoid these problems, a product cost estimation system should track prototype component costs separately from production costs. Without this feature, it is difficult to avoid accidentally inflating production cost estimates with prototype costs.*
>
> — "The Arena Solutions Guide to Outsourcing: Removing Barriers, Maintaining Boundaries," Arena Solutions, 2011

The security aspect of collaboration in the BMMS is of specific importance, not only—as one may initially expect—because of the privacy provided to the OEM. In fact, security is a benefit to the suppliers as well because the security features of the BMMS enhance the comfort level of the suppliers, as is described in the following quote from Arena:

> *OEMs often need to collect competitive quotes from multiple contract manufacturers during the sourcing process. Traditionally, this procedure involves producing duplicate copies of full product documentation followed by a bidding phase where detailed quote information is gathered. In the meantime, if any part specifications change, the updated information must be packaged and re-sent to each manufacturer. With Arena, there is a single instance of the product data available online and always up-to-date. Access is granted electronically so there is no printing, shipping or faxing. The contract manufacturers invited to the workspace can't see one another's quote information, so the OEM retains privacy and*

> *control. And the OEM has confidence that the competitive bids are truly competitive—that is based on the same product specification information. Soliciting bids is greatly simplified to a process of setting up access privileges and e-mailing a link to the appropriate part or assembly to potential suppliers.*
>
> *—" The Arena Solutions Guide to Outsourcing: Removing Barriers, Maintaining Boundaries," Arena Solutions, 2011*

Again, these are simply features that make the OEM more desirable to work with in the eyes of suppliers and contract manufacturers. BOMs differ in their design depending upon their area and usage. When we think of a single uniform "BOM," it's important to remember that BOMs, in fact, have many different requirements depending upon their purpose, and the various individuals that interact with the BOM need to see the BOM differently. The most obvious difference is between the engineering BOM (EBOM) and the manufacturing BOM (MBOM) that have been discussed; however there are many other types of BOMs, as is described below:

> *For in-house engineering use, BOM structure may vary based on the engineering discipline. Designers and mechanical engineers often prefer a BOM with nested sub-assemblies as the sub-assemblies can be leveraged across various product designs. In these cases, the BOM often depicts custom designed components and provides critical information about the structure of the product. Electrical engineers, on the other hand, prefer BOMs that are not nested as they generally capture off-the-shelf components. Here, the way in which the components are wired together (the schematic) is important to the engineer, but not to the overall structure of the bills of materials.*
>
> *— "The Arena Solutions Guide to Outsourcing: Removing Barriers, Maintaining Boundaries," Arena Solutions, 2011*

While nested BOMs, as explained to people, have the reputation for being an albatross (which is highly dependent upon the use of older technology for managing the BOMs), they provide a great advantage for collaboration with various partners. Many supply chain consultants talk about flatting the BOM, but representing the levels in the BOM has tremendous advantages for collaboration.

When sharing BOMs with a contract manufacturer, partner or collaborator, it can be helpful to use a BOM with some structure. Nesting and creating sub-assemblies within your BOM allows you to isolate specific sub-assemblies, so you can share only the design data that you need your partner to see. If your partner is helping you with a design, you might choose to share just the sub-assembly that relates to their work, thereby protecting the intellectual property associated with the other aspects of the product design.

A multi-level BOM is also helpful when you have complex and highly configurable products. Updating a sub-assembly within a larger product assembly can be done quickly, if you have structured your BOM as multi-leveled, since a change order only needs to address a subset of the product. The sub-assembly can be revised and used in multiple higher-level assemblies as necessary. The higher-level assemblies only need to be revised as far up the product structure tree as form, fit and function rules dictate.

A multi-level BOM can also reduce risk when you have products that use parts with long lead times, high inventory costs, or single source vendors. A BOM with sub-assemblies allows your operations group to pinpoint potential alternatives to expensive parts and provides better visibility into assemblies and sub-assemblies that may require extra work.

—"Managing Multi Level BOMs," Arena Solutions

Customers of the BOM

One issue has always challenged good BOM management: the fact that there are so many customers of the BOM. This quote is from *Bills of Material for a Lean Enterprise:*

> *Everybody in the company uses the bill of material. No single area of the company owns the bill. Manufacturing would make changes in the bill that would have long-term engineering or product liability repercussions. Over a period of years, we had demonstrated that*

even if manufacturing requested a change in the bill, we wouldn't make it. So manufacturing made their own bill of material and it happened to be documented on a corkboard in the stockroom. Obviously, Manufacturing uses the bill of material to build a product. If it doesn't have access to the "real" bill of material, it'll make their own BOM. The bill is also used to help determine the routing, that is, how to make the product. Finance and accounting use the bill to cost the product. Order entry uses the bill of material to help configure the product. The service department needs the bill to know which service parts go into the product. Finally, quality assurance uses the bill to assure the product is made properly. These are the "customers" of the bill of material structuring process. Each customer has his or her own expectations for the product of the process. Everyone wants the bill structured to suit his or her own needs and that's why the fight starts.

Providing information to so many groups in the way they want to see it is challenging; however, some BMMS vendors have met the challenge. The right BMMS can provide unique representations of the BOM to all these diverse groups. A BMMS makes it unnecessary to set up BOM management in shared systems in a way that only satisfies one group. It also makes it unnecessary for each group to maintain its own separate BOM management system, each of which is updated without communicating to the other systems. The groups that use BOM information do not coordinate effectively, and instead tend to "throw things over the wall."

Enabling Collaboration from the Ground Up

What should be apparent from the above is that the needs of a highly collaborative and controllable BMMS cannot be met by general software that was never designed to meet those needs. Whenever a company already has software based on an older design, it is motivated to try to make small changes to the software to make it meet a different purpose. However, the underlying design of an application is quite important. From the very start, an application must be designed with the intent of meeting the objectives in mind. I have seen many examples of this through the years. For instance, in demand planning, many companies have attempted to add on or "graft" attribute forecasting capabilities to a system that was already designed with a static hierarchy. The result is not competitive with solutions that were designed originally with attribute-based capabilities. For those interested, this is described in detail in the post below:

http://www.scmfocus.com/demandplanning/2010/07/pivot-forecasting-renders-forecast-hierarchies-obsolete/

Competitive pressure exerted by smaller and more innovative software companies on the large monopoly vendors in the enterprise market is due, in fact, to business processes that need very specific functionality combined with factors such as hardware and software innovations that allow a niche vendor to develop a superior solution. In order for smaller companies to have any chance of competing, they must offer significantly superior solutions. Without better solutions, the advantages that come with size—such as marketing, conference coverage, partnership opportunities with major consulting firms, application integration considerations, analyst coverage and a host of other benefits— tilt the playing field heavily in the direction of the larger vendors.

Larger vendors, on the other hand, can significantly lag applications that have been designed for a specific process for years, slowly co-opting the language of the particular innovation, making some small code changes to partially cover the functionality in question, and generally attempting to introduce ideas generated by the smaller innovative companies into their products. One example of this is found with SAP with respect to inventory optimization and multi-echelon planning, which I have described in the article posted below:

http://www.scmfocus.com/inventoryoptimizationmultiechelon/2011/04/sap-is-about-to-change-its-inventory-optimization-story/

A number of years ago, SAP tried to do something similar with its material master, and with some slight coding adjustments, pitched the extremely basic functionality as a content management solution (CMS). This fooled some executive decision makers, but it really should not have because the material master functionality is about as divorced from a CMS as could be. With this "CMS" functionality, they then took pre-existing life cycle functionality that was distributed across a variety of applications and proceeded to state that they had a "PLM" system, which as I have already discussed, does not make very much sense. What really changed? Not much of anything. Essentially they rebranded existing functionality(which was not a BOM management system nor integrated lifecycle functionality) into PLM.

This was one the of the more brazen attempts of product adjustment I have witnessed, as the material master is not designed to hold the media files necessary for a BMMS. Without the media files, the system can never be integrated with design and engineering. As I have said, in many cases the major vendors are successful in co-opting the new area with inappropriate functionality, but in this case the stretch was simply too large, and SAP no longer actively markets their "content management solution." After running into problematic and nonfunctional SAP PLM implementations on several occasions (one client told me, "that is our PLM server, it just sits unused in the corner"), I wrote an article questioning if SAP's PLM solution actually ever existed.

http://www.scmfocus.com/servicepartsplanning/2009/04/21/is-sap-plm-for-real/

Undaunted, SAP worked with an engineering and design software vendor called Right Hemisphere, whom they finally purchased. Although SAP touts this solution as a PLM solution, CAD or 3D visualization software is not part of the BMMS. Instead, CAD systems provide input to the BMMS, meaning that your selection of a BMMS has the potential to control your selection of a CAD solution, which should not happen. Furthermore, most companies already selected their CAD systems and have been using them for years. For them, migrating to Right Hemisphere just to use SAP's PLM solution makes little sense. In contrast, the applications of Arena Solutions and Agile do not require a specific CAD application. They can hold the CAD files of any system, as was described in Chapter 3: "The Bill of Materials (EBOM) in the Design and Engineering Systems."

SAP has also thrown in Business Objects reporting, which can report off of their "PLM solution." This is a problem because a BMMS should not need an external reporting system, but should be searchable from within the application, as I have shown repeatedly with the search capabilities of Arena Solutions. Therefore, the new SAP PLM solution is problematic for a number of reasons:

1. Design and CAD systems are not part of the BMMS.

2. A material master is still not a CSM.

3. A BMMS should not require an external reporting system, but should be able to meet all search requirements from within the application.

Executives who are presented with SAP's "PLM solution" will end up confused as to what a BMMS is. SAP seems to be cobbling together its PLM solution from various parts, which when combined do not make a BMMS. The end result will be more confusion in the marketplace regarding the definition of a BMMS. SAP is so large and influential that they can influence how companies think of application categories, even if their model is incorrect. This prompted me to write a second article to question once again whether SAP actually has a PLM solution.

http://www.scmfocus.com/billofmaterials/2012/04/08/does-sap-finally-have-a-plm-solution/

I have written some of the more outspoken articles on SAP's *faux* BMMS/PLM solution. However, few people that write articles on the web are willing to criticize SAP primarily because most people that know much about SAP— and even many that don't—derive some type of income from SAP (either consulting revenue or advertising). Therefore, SAP can say pretty much anything it likes knowing that the vast majority of information outlets on the Internet will line up and support them and its vision. SAP can also bring out a limited-function solution and face no negative media. When I search for articles on the Internet about SAP, the only critical commentary I can find are comments left on articles, not within the articles themselves.

Taking old functionality and repurposing it is nothing new in the enterprise software space, and can be enough to trick executive decision makers who don't want to deal with a large number of vendors. If a company already deals with a large software vendor and that vendor puts together some semblance of a solution (no matter how inferior), that solution will be appealing to executive decision makers who are adverse to switching vendors.

Arena Solutions has witnessed many of the same types of activities that I have in various vendors that have entered the PLM space. I know this from speaking with them, and from at least one statement in their publications, such as the following:

> *The need for more sophisticated collaboration tools is compelling enough that many solutions have sprung up to try to fill it. But many of these solutions attempt to adapt existing product data management platforms to a collaborative environment, an undertaking that involves* enormous re-engineering *to create access to an inherently closed system. Naturally, these costs are passed on to clients.*
>
> — Arena Solutions

Here Arena uses a key phrase, which is "enormous re-engineering." As soon as the term re-engineering or repurposing is used within the context of software, one should tread very carefully. Enterprise software generally does not re-engineer or repurpose very well. Here is an example of why this is the case:

The spreadsheet is one of the most flexible applications ever invented; in fact, it's the ultimate blank slate. It can be used for a wide variety of activities and my spreadsheets span the continuum from simple tables to large multi-tabbed monsters with complex formulas. For the first few years that I worked in consulting, I primarily built supply chain analysis spreadsheets that allowed me to incorporate all types of supply chain calculations without having to know how to code. The same Excel program has been used to do everything from financial analysis to calculating the change in rotation in planets (a spreadsheet that came with a book on advanced uses of Excel). The reason Excel—and spreadsheets in general—can have such a broad application is because the software is not customized for any one use. A spreadsheet is an unstructured, generalized application; it is part word processor, part calculator, and part multi-tabbed table management system. It does not support any particular business process, and that is where its immense flexibility comes from. In addition to being an application, its built-in macros, many formulas, and innumerable third party plug-ins essentially make Excel its own development environment.

However, enterprise software does not work this way because an enterprise application is directed toward a specific purpose. Its user interface, business logic and data layer are all customized for that purpose, which is why repurposing enterprise software typically does not work very well. Repurposing is, in essence, an attempt by the software vendor to get more sales from the same code base, but in the vast majority of cases repurposing does not do very much for the customer. In fact, many enterprise applications are customized for a particular industry environment and may not transition very well to other industries. This is certainly the case with production planning and scheduling software, where software designed for discrete manufacturing typically does not translate very well to process manufacturing.

http://www.scmfocus.com/productionplanningandscheduling/2011/03/09/how-process-manufacturing-differs-from-discrete-manufacturing-and-how-this-relates-to-software-selection/

In light of what I have written above, the rule those making a BMMS software selection should apply is that any application, which claims BMMS-type functionality, must have this functionality not as an adjunct to its main functionality, but must be specifically designed from the ground up with all of the functionalities described up to this point.

BOM Data and Related Data

In addition to the text fields in the BOM, a BMMS contains the data files that are related to the BOM. For example, a design document or the approved suppliers for a part in a BOM are not technically part of the BOM, but are still contained in the BMMS. Technically, the BOM is simply the listing...

> *...of the raw materials, sub-assemblies, intermediate assemblies, sub-components, components, parts and the quantities of each needed to manufacture an end product.*
>
> — Wikipedia

To leverage the related information properly, it is necessary for the BMMS to be able to integrate all of the associated files with the BOM. This truly integrated solution, where every piece of information related to the BOM is held and is accessible within one system, essentially replaces the file folder approach to managing these files. A rich application experience is created with the types of information that both the implementer of the software and their partners want to see, including the following:

1. The BOM

2. The approved vendor/supplier list per part

3. Pricing and quoting information per part

4. Design/CAD documents

5. Design specifications

6. The status of the BOM (in design, in production, etc.)

7. The item category

8. The individuals associated with each BOM

Importing Data into Arena Solutions

Getting data into the application is the first step to using a BMMS, something which Arena Solutions makes very straightforward. My previous experience with an application called Demand Works Smoothie has demonstrated clearly to me that a best practice is the ability to load enterprise applications from spreadsheets. There are many advantages to being able to do this, one being that the task can be performed by business resources rather than having to go through IT, which always takes longer and greatly limits the freedom that that business has with using the application. This topic is covered in detail the post below:

http://www.scmfocus.com/supplychainmasterdata/2010/09/why-demand-works-is-a-model-for-configutationdata-management/

It turns out that Arena Solutions has been similarly well thought out in this regard.

Arena has templates that can be downloaded directly from the application online, which can be used to import all the different types of data that makes Arena Solutions work. Arena recommends importing in "layers" so that different types of data are imported into the model in a particular sequence. Because the import functionality is so strong, Arena implementations tend to progress quickly from the data perspective.

more? Learn how to get started with Arena in less than 5 days for as little as $99/user per month.

BOM and Items Import Column Requirements

Arena Solutions, Inc [US] https://**app.bom.com**/bom-import/import-help?guidelines_mode_p=0

Column Requirements

▪ **required** for all imports; at least one of the two must be completed.

▪ **required** only when importing a bill of materials.

▪ **optional** but only imported when importing a bill of materials.

* **required** for this workspace. When importing new Items (or existing Items with no values assigned for these fields), these columns must be included with a value entered for each Item.

▪ **either/or** required when importing source relationships. Use the lighter green columns to specify the same source relationships for production and prototype sourcing **or** the darker green columns to specify different source relationships for production and prototype sourcing. **Please note** that if data is entered in both columns, the data in the darker green columns will override data in the lighter green columns.

Column Name	Format	Example
level	Number, top level is **0**	0
line_number	Any number	10
reference_designator	Any text string. (Maximum length: 32000)	R1, R2, R3, C1, C2
bom_notes	Any text string. (Maximum length: 4000)	30 minutes heating time
quantity	Any valid number	2.5
item_name	Any text string. (Maximum length: 100)	Tantalum Capacitor
item_number	Any text string. (Maximum length: 200)	856-0026
revision	Any text string. (Maximum length: 15)	A
item_category	Any text string. (Maximum length: 4000)	Capacitor
item_category_path	Any text string. (Maximum length: 4000)	Part\Capacitor
description	Any text string. (Maximum length: 4000)	Tantalum Capacitor 56880-5767
owner	Any text string. (Maximum length: 50)	Eric
procurement_type	Valid entries (numeric and string entries are both acceptable):	OTS

In order to format the columns correctly, Arena offers this guide, which is opened by selecting the import guidelines.

◇	A	B	C	D	E	F	G	H	I	J
			Sheets	Charts	SmartArt Graphics	WordArt				
1	Part Number	Item_Name	Revision	Unit_Of_Measure	Item_Category	Resistance	Power	Capacitance	Voltage	Footprint
2	120-00010	CAP 100UF 6.3V CERAMIC Y5V 1206	A	EA	Capacitor			100 uF	6.3 V	1206
3	120-00011	CAP 22UF 25V CERAMIC X5R 1210	B	EA	Capacitor			22 uF	25 V	1210
4	120-00012	CAP 4.7UF 6.3V CERAMIC X5R 0603	B	EA	Capacitr			4.7 uF	6.3 V	'0603
5	120-00013	CAP 10UF 6.3V CERAMIC X5R 0603	A	EA	Capacitor			10 uF	6.3 V	'0603
6	120-00014	CAP 330UF 4.0V ELECT POLY 1240 SMD	A	EA	Capacitor			330 uF	4 V	'1240
7	180-00008	RES 120 OHM 1/16W .5% 0402 SMD	A	EA	Resistor	120 Ohm	1/16 W			'0402
8	180-00009	RES 130 OHM 1/16W .5% 0402 SMD		1 EA	Resistor	130 Ohm	1/16 W			'0402
9	180-00002			2 EA	Resistor	82 Ohm	1/16 W			'0603
10	180-00011	RES 1.2K OHM 1/16W 5% 0402 SMD	A	EA	Resistor	1.2K Ohm	1/16 W			'0402
11	180-00001	RES 1.6K OHM 1/16W 5% 0402 SMD	E	EA	Resistor	1.6K Ohm	1/16 W			'0402

This shows a specific format with some data populated.

Once the file is formatted properly, it can be imported with this utility, followed by a mapping and error checking utility that prevents incorrectly-formatted data from being brought into the application. Several attempts might be required to get the format correct. However, once the format is correct a very large amount of data can be imported into Arena very quickly.

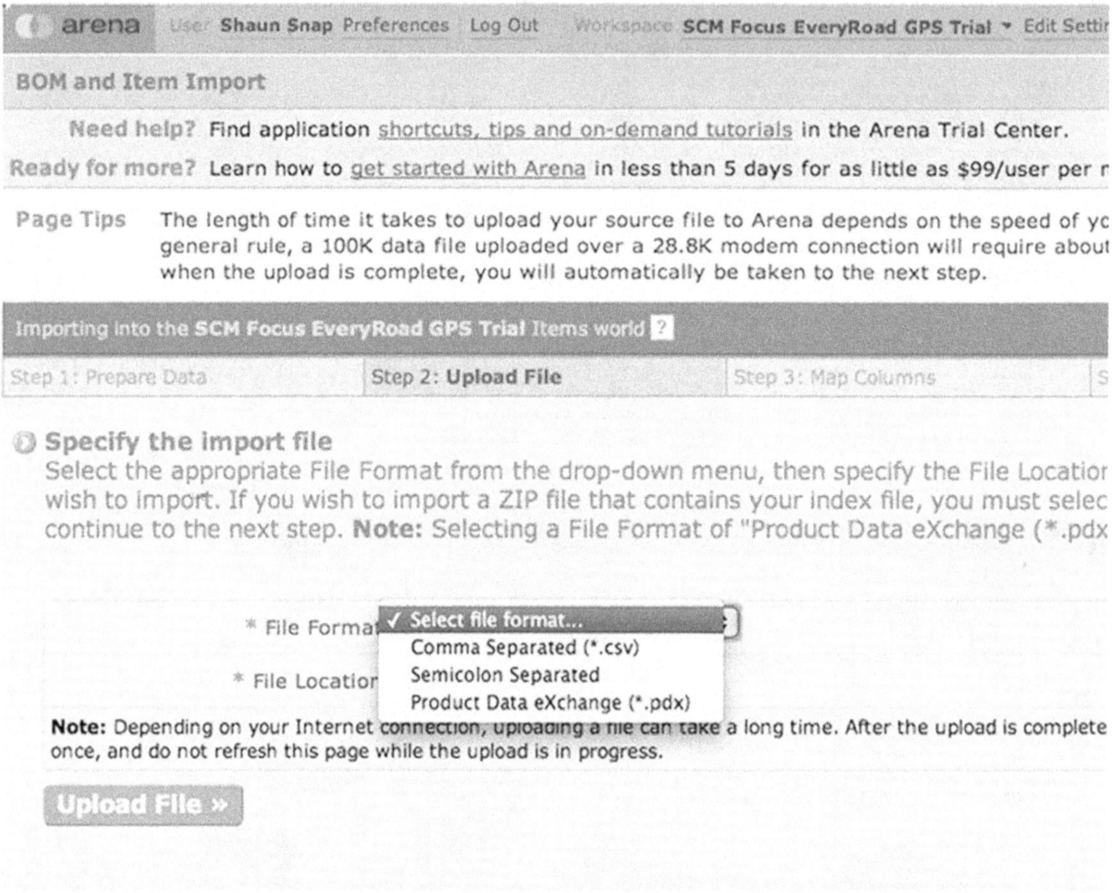

As can be seen above, there are several options for format type; common ones include CSV (which is often used to export data from Excel or even from a database) and PDX format. PDX is not an Arena proprietary format, but instead is "an international electronics manufacturing initiative (iNEMI) standard, and is the industry standard for file sharing in manufacturing." It is considered the "the cleanest and most secure way for OEMs and suppliers to share build kits, BOM data and quote packages"—"PDX Viewer,"—Arena Solutions. Therefore, while the other file formats essentially are used to build the BOM database from flat files, PDX is sort of a prebaked file format for BOMs. Secondly, the BMMS is not the only way to view the PDX. Instead, Arena has provided a PDX viewer. This is shown on the following page:

Level	Item Number	Rev	Item Name
1	▾ 20-0015	A	EveryRoad, PCBA
2	40-0035	A	EveryRoad, Circuit Board
2	40-0038	A	GPS Micro controller
2	40-0039	A	USB Connector
2	40-0041	A	0.1uF Ceramic Chip Capacitor
2	40-0042	A	10k Resistor
1	50-0016	A	EveryRoad, Rear Panel
1	50-0019	A	Screw, M2 x 5, ST, PH

An individual may view the PDX format without having a specific BMMS. This can allow companies to easily view BOM information without having to log in to another company's application. Of course, this also means that changes cannot be made to the BOM information that would also persist in the application.

Understanding PLM Versus BOM Management Solutions

Without understanding the definitions of lifecycle, PLM and BOM management, good decisions regarding the acquisition and deployment of the software in these categories are very difficult to make. Confusion between the different terms and functionalities prevents companies from getting the appropriate solutions to improve how they manage the BOM. When comparing "PLM" and BOM management solutions, it's important to ask software vendors these questions:

1. Is the solution primarily focused on managing the material and BOM objects or something else?

2. Is the solution presented as a separate application, or as functionality that is distributed throughout the larger ERP suite?

3. PLM and BOM management are not the same thing. Ask for an explanation as to what central problem the software is trying to solve, and then how the software solves it. For instance, the solution offered by SAP does not address BOM management and incorporates areas of functionality and a CAD application related to engineering and design, which is not part of BOM management. Some of the solutions offered in this space simply don't make any sense. They are the result of a software vendor cobbling together a product with whatever is handy, and pushing it out even though it doesn't actually meet the real requirements of BOM management. The fact that a PLM vendor happens to be the same software vendor that makes the company's current ERP system is not a good enough reason to select their application, particularly if they have a low probability of meeting the business requirements. Attention to business requirements detail is important for all software selections, but is of particular importance in the BMMS/PLM market.

4. How strong are the collaborative capabilities of the software? BOM management requirements are inherently collaborative and outside parties in particular must be able to quickly and easily use the application. The standard has already been set by Arena Solutions in this area, and acceptance of a lower level of collaboration functionality must be well-justified. Other factors, such as the functionality of the application's BOM workflow as well as the BMMS's user-friendliness, are far more important to the success of the BMMS implementation than whether the ERP company has some adapters that can be used by the implementing company. In fact, the lesson from collaboration projects is that unless the software is easy to use, it generally won't be used very much, and fewer benefits will be realized. The collaborative capability of BMMS software can't be just average; it must be exceptional. These questions and approach to thinking can help anyone understand what they are appraising when evaluating this classification of software. The ease of setting up access to their BMMS is described by Arena Solutions on the following page:

There are no remote users who need a special password or a VPN to use the system; there are no client applications that need to be installed at each user's computer. The system provides consistent access to everyone regardless of location.
— "Collaborative Tools for Product Development: A New Approach,"
Arena Solutions, 2011

The Collaborative Aspects of the BOM

The amount of true supply chain collaboration is far below that which is generally discussed and written about. The shortage of application-based supply chain collaboration projects is evident in the lack of development effort that has been put into collaboration software. In fact, as I described in the book *Supply Chain Forecasting Software*:

For all the discussion about the importance of collaboration across the supply chain and how much opportunity there is to share information by web applications, it is interesting to note how much of a typical company's collaboration is still based upon EDI transactions. However, the fact that EDI information is passed between partners does not necessarily mean the data is used, and while collaboration on objects such as advanced shipment notifications and purchase orders is now commonplace, companies have been slow to move outside of what are essentially transactional objects and into planning objects like forecasts. Information sharing is certainly not limited by technology, and every year the technological barriers fall a bit more. Instead, it is limited, in part, by the relationships between buyers and suppliers, which are as much competitive as collaborative. This fact is left out of many white papers, conference presentations and books on the topic.

This is why, despite all of the discussion about supply chain collaboration with respect to things like forecasting and purchase orders, in my view the best collaboration software was developed not in the supply chain collaboration space, but in the BOM management space.

Understanding Arena's Authorization or Permissions Model

We have discussed the importance of the BMMS's authorization model several times, but have alluded to it in general terms only. Now is a good time to explain how a BMMS solution's authorization model should work.

An application's authorization model is what allows system users to perform various activities in the system. The BMMS must have a very strong but also nuanced authorization model. The following statement from Wikipedia is a nice description of an authorization model:

> *Most modern, multi-user operating systems include access control and thereby rely on authorization. Access control also makes use of authentication to verify the identity of consumers. When a consumer tries to access a resource, the access control process checks that the consumer has been authorized to use that resource.*
>
> — Wikipedia

However, this definition—as well as other quotations and many of the books in this area—miss out on how much authorizations have changed over the years. In order to understand the history of authorization models more fully, I have provided some examples from the following software areas:

1. Authorization in Operating Systems

2. Authorization in SAP

3. Authorization in Arena Solutions

Authorization in the Operating Systems

Authorization models are necessary for all types of software, and there is a strong tendency in many applications—both consumer and enterprise—to increase the sophistication of the authorization model expected benefits. In its early stages of development, the UNIX operating system had strong authorization with security. Most other operating systems significantly lagged UNIX's authorizations. In UNIX, permission or authorization is set at the user, file and directory levels.

UNIX was considered the most secure operating system, and probably still is, although many of its features have been copied. Operating systems that were designed for the desktop rather than for the server environment were originally developed without much in the way of authorization. However, even PC operating systems eventually added authorization. For instance, Apple computers had, in my opinion, the first effective multi-user authorization system in a graphical operating system environment. I show examples of this system below:

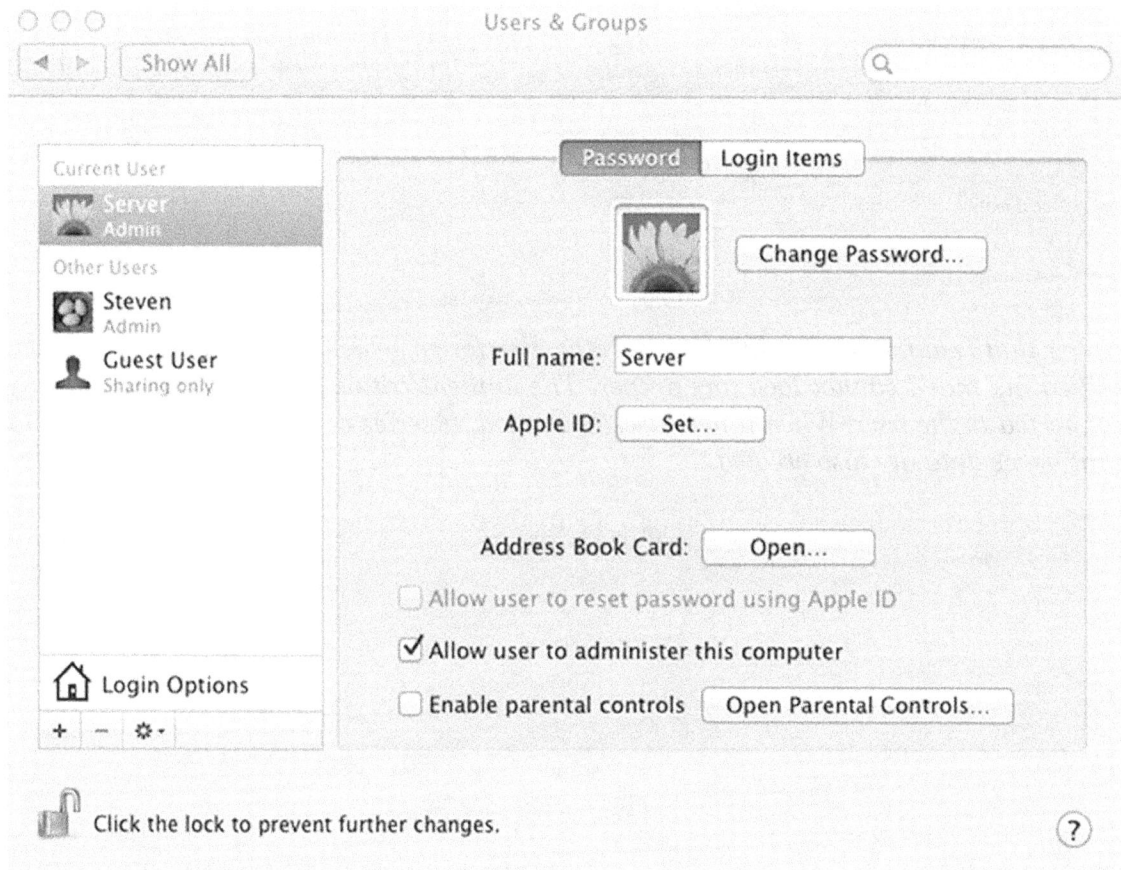

Multiple users can be set up to use a single computer, and this creates a separate space for each user. Aside from the other users that show in the drop down menu, the user is mostly unaware of the computer's other users because their settings are never changed.

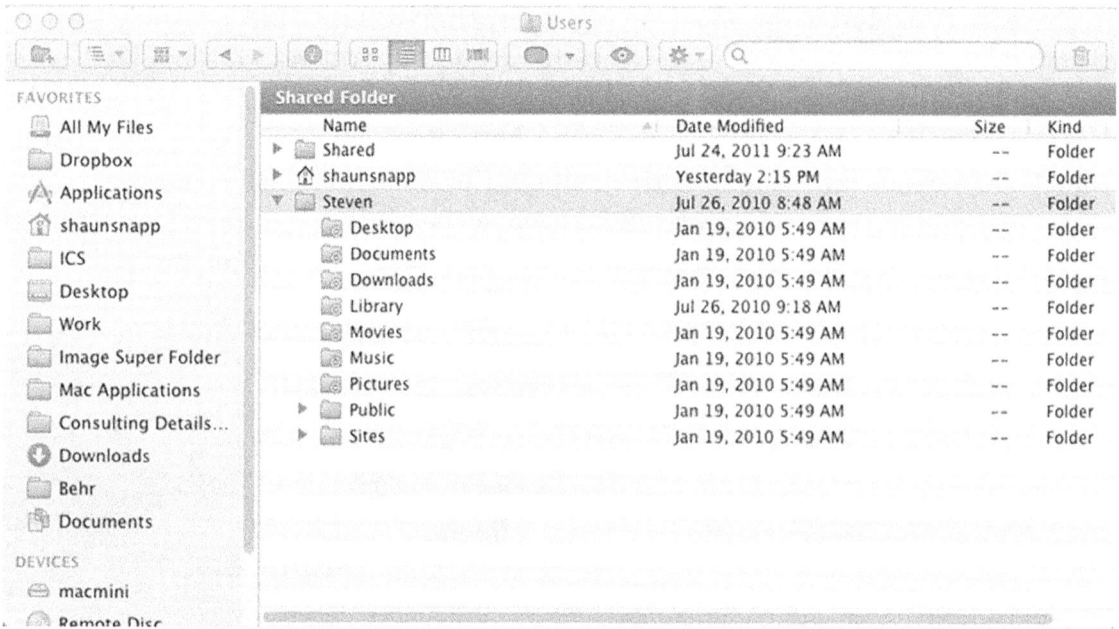

Notice that I cannot see Steven's files, only the directories, which have red circles on them, indicating that I cannot look any deeper. The authentication is simple and is directly connected to the user. When a new user is created, a series of folders designed to hold that user's data are also created.

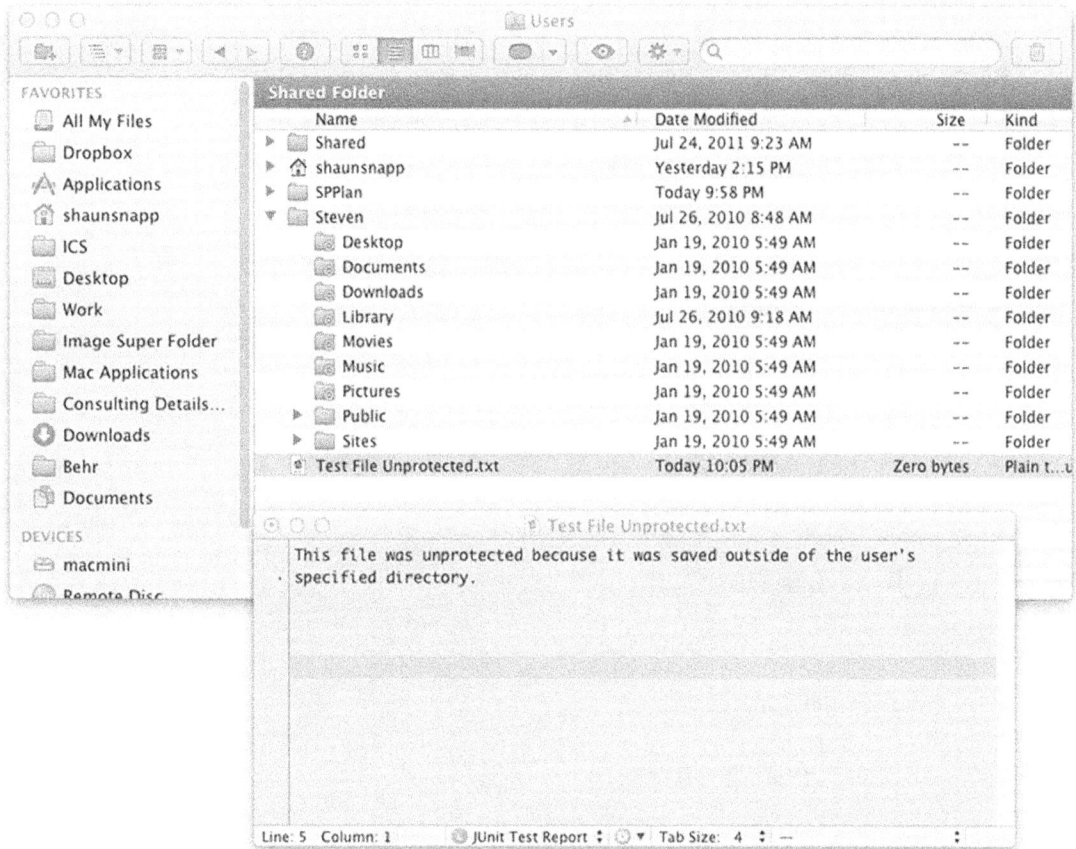

However, notice that if Steven saved a file outside his authenticated directories, say in the root of the user directory, and named the file "Test File Unprotected," I could then open the file. This is called "user controlled file authorization," and works well for the purpose of a multi-user operating system. Each user must simply remember to save their files in their own protected folders.

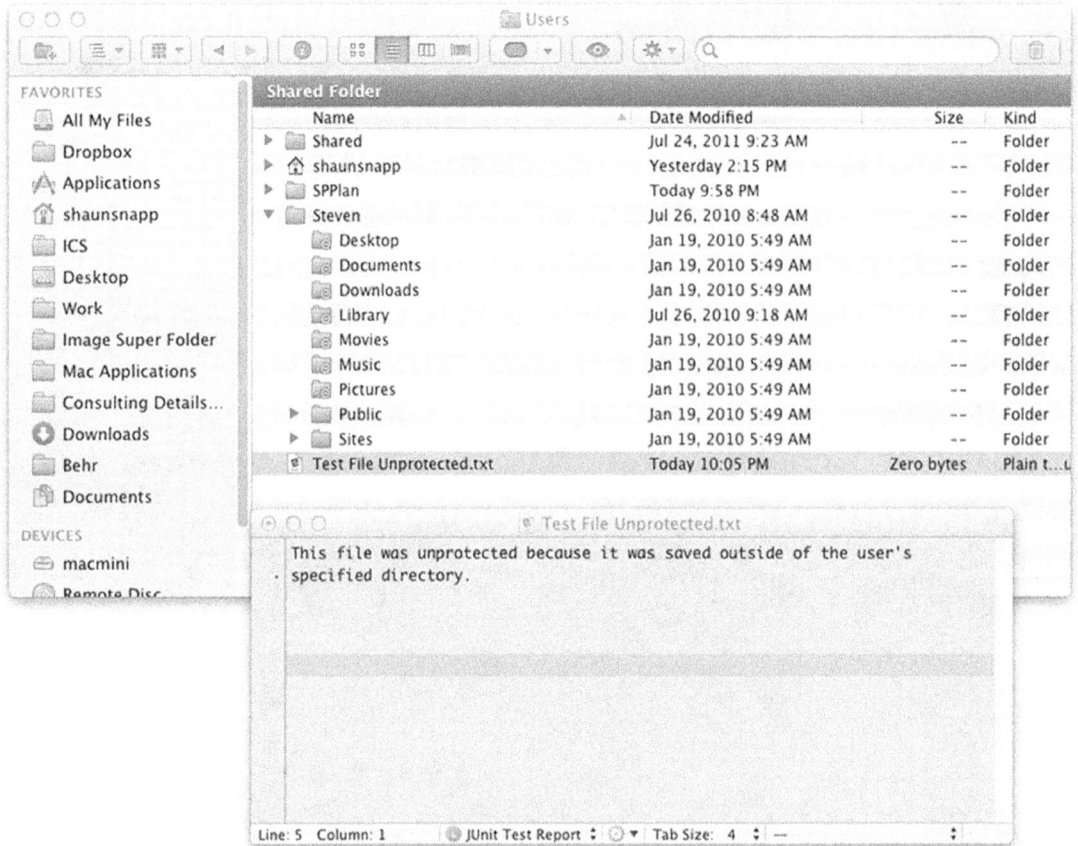

In the Mac operating system (which also happens to be built upon a UNIX base), we can see more detail about the file permissions by performing a right mouse click and selecting "Show Info." Here we can see that anyone can read the file (if they can access it; if it has been saved in a private directory it cannot be accessed), but only the owner can write or change it. Outside of that, all permissions are restricted. Simply selecting the box and then entering the authorization code can enable changes.

Authorization functionality can be interpreted from a number of angles. Part of defining authorization is simply to consider what actions are possible. In this example, nine options can be set for the file in terms of read, write and execute. However, there are actually many more options. The default option is just as important as the number of options. The authorization model could be considered as the combinations of options (which could be considered the depth of the authorization model) combined with the configuration of what options are turned on or off under certain circumstances.

The functionality that you have seen allows multiple users to use the same computer seamlessly. This made the Apple operating system both more secure and more functional. Authorization is one of those things that can seem to be not a key differentiator at first glance, but which places a ceiling on the future capabilities of the application, how it can be used, and how it can be shared. Microsoft copied aspects of Apple's multi-user authentication, but their system was always less reliable. Far fewer people use Windows in multi-user mode per machine than use Apple. Authorization is still a clear advantage for Apple, enabling more privacy and higher utilization of one computer than a Windows machine.

Authorization in SAP

Understanding authorization in SAP is a very important step toward understanding enterprise software authorization. SAP's authorization model is complex, and this section is designed to explain how authorization in an established and well-known system differs with the authorization in a BMMS. Therefore, for those with a background in SAP security, forgive some of the oversimplifications that I have been required to make in order to keep this topic a manageable length.

SAP's BOM Authorization

SAP recognized that the BOM needs to have a special authorization design. They actually have four different authorizations for the BOM:

- General Authorization for Processing BOMs

- Authorization for Object in BOM Plant

- Authorization to Process BOM without Charge Number

- Authorization for Mass Changes

- Authorization for Variable Lists

These authorizations may allow one user to create a BOM in some plants, but not others. Another authorization may allow a user to maintain a BOM without a change number, or allow some users to make mass changes to BOMs while other users can only make one change at a time.

However, while this is a level of authorization that does allow for some small shades of grey, it is still far too broad, and in effect does nothing to make the BOM a collaborative object. It does not enable part of the BOM to be changed, while restricting other parts of the BOM, and this authorization capability is critical to the BOM authorization requirements at companies all over the world. To see how BOM authorization should be setup, lets move into the next section.

Authorization in Arena Solutions

Arena Solutions differs from SAP in that it was designed from the outset to be accessed by many individuals both inside and outside of the company. In fact, because Arena Solutions is SaaS based, the application server itself is outside of the company that "owns it." Arena Solutions also has the most forward-thinking authorization model that I have seen. Arena is able to set up users on its demo system very easily. Of course, a demo system does not need to be very secure; however, I have been using the Arena demo system for several years off and on, and interestingly I never seem to have a problem with Arena system administrators even though I am not paying them to use the system. That is, I would expect much more responsiveness from SAP security specialists, as I am interacting with them on a real project and they are being paid to support SAP users. However, that is the fact of what I have observed with respect to service discrepancies.

The Arena Solutions authorization model is incredibly detailed, yet surprisingly simple to configure. For example, it allows suppliers who interact with their SaaS software to see only what they are allowed to see by their authorization level. A product may be made up of thousands of parts, but an outside supplier may only be able to see one of the parts when they log in to the application. The authorization model is not simply based upon a transaction as in SAP, as is explained by displaying the indented BOM screen below:

Arena's authorization allows the administrator to pick and choose which parts will be shared with which internal and external users.

New Employee

Creating a New Employee ?   Cancel

Step 1: **Create Profile**   Step 2: Select Workspaces   Step 3: Assign Access Roles

Enter the information for the new Employee below and click **Create Profile**.

* denotes a required field

Personal Information

* First Name	Steven
* Last Name	Miller
* Email Address	supplychainplan@gmail.com
* Temporary Password	••••••••

Passwords must be 6-18 characters in length and contain at least one letter and one number.

* Confirm Temporary Password	••••••••

Passwords must be 6-18 characters in length and contain at least one letter and one number.

* Administrator	No ⬍

Select **Yes** to allow this Employee to administer your Arena account.

* Status	Enabled ⬍

Select **Disabled** to deactivate this Employee without disturbing existing work.

Email New Employee	☐ (Check this box to have the newly created account information sent to this Employee.)

Passwords must be 6-18 characters in length and contain at least one letter and one number.

External Accounts

Skype Name	

In the Skype interface, make sure that your privacy settings allow your status to be shown on the web (otherwise, users will not be able to see whether you're online).

Create Profile »

Here I am creating a profile.

Details for
New Employee

Creating a New Employee ?   « Back   Cancel

Step 1: Create Profile   Step 2: Select Workspaces   Step 3: **Assign Access Roles**

Select an **access role and initial workspace** for this new user and click **Assign Access Roles**.

1 Workspaces

#	Workspace	Description		Initial Workspace
01	SCM Focus EveryRoad GPS Trial	This workspace contains prepopulated sample data for EveryRoad GPS car navigation systems with trial user modifications.	Approver Employee [Read-Only, No Cost Visibility] / Approver Employee [Read-Only] / ✓ Full Employee [Design Revision Creation] / Full Employee [No Revision Creation, Buyer] / Full Employee [No Revision Creation, No Cost Visibility] / Full Employee [No Revision Creation] / Full Employee [Production Revision Creation] / Read-Only Employee [No Approval, No Cost Visibility] / Read-Only Employee [No Approval]	⦿

Assign Access Roles »

« Back   Cancel

Arena Release 94
Copyright 2001-2012, Arena Solutions. All rights reserved.

Arena Support
Have a question, problem or product idea?
Let us know!

FastFeedback »

I set the authorization level of the user. Here the concept of a "Workspace" is introduced. The workspace is the area where users are assigned so they can work with Arena.

I can assign different users to different workspaces.

There are any number of workspaces that exist within Arena. Workspaces are separately archived.

The Power of This Authorization Model

Without an efficient and nuanced authorization model, a company could not open its application to other partners, and the application would be a much weaker value proposition. The need for many applications to become more collaborative means that more companies will have the employees of other companies logging into and using their applications; authorization is ever more important. I tried explaining the importance of a flexible authorization model to a software vendor with whom I consulted. They were redesigning their application, and for whatever reason I was not able to communicate to them how important this feature is. One problem was that their application tended to be sold into smaller companies that did not have users logging in who were external to the company. In these types of environments, authorization and controls tend to be less important.

When this vendor originally developed its solution, no one had really heard of what I described above. Instead, each application was inward-looking, authorization was chiefly for internal employees, and data was exchanged primarily through extraction and importation (i.e., EDI). The software vendor never developed an effective permission model, and in fact the reasons for not doing so, which may include the reasons I listed above, should be strategically analyzed with consideration for what other best-of-breed software vendors have accomplished with their enhanced authorization models.

Allowing Intelligent Input from Supply Chain Partners

A major selling point for Arena Solutions' software is the ability for partners to interact with and make adjustments to data for which they are a subject matter expert. They have run circles around Oracle and SAP in this area. While SAP has a robust internal authorization model, it lags behind Arena Solutions, even though SAP is the largest and best-known enterprise software vendor and Arena is relatively unknown outside of BOM management circles. Conceptually SAP is stuck in the past, where the ERP system was internally focused. Issues with the authorization model are not restricted to SAP ERP, as the supply chain planning SAP APO system (around thirteen years old, about as old as Arena Solutions) uses the same authorization model. The authorization model has created a serious problem for SAP as they try to make their software more collaborative but with little success. This is due to two major factors:

1. The structure of the software's authorization model

2. The user interface, or SAPGUI, is not designed to be shared outside of one enterprise.

In order to interact with suppliers, SAP must create a special "collaborative" section of the application, which allows suppliers to log in. Two application interfaces are necessary: one thick client for the internal users and one thin client for the external users.

In addition, the HMTL portion of SAP's interface is far inferior to that of Arena Solutions. I am increasingly of the opinion that HMTL interfaces (assisted by a few supporting technologies like Java) are the way to go, particularly in supply chain applications. Supply chain applications are often not designed to be collaborative (or even thought be collaborative). However, if we take an example like production planning and scheduling, it is clear that allowing users from outside the company to have access can improve the plan, especially when outside companies are performing the production, which increasingly is the case. In situations where the production is planned for contract manufacturers, having a unified HTML interface with an effective authorization model can allow the contract manufacturer to make changes to aspects of the production plan (such as just their location) that can provide great benefit to the main implementation company or the OEM. This type of collaboration is quite feasible with an HTML-based application like PlanetTogether.

The synopsis of this story is that most supply chain applications are not collaborative, which is more a function of the design of these applications than the actual need for collaboration in each of the application areas. That is, the design of supply chain applications tends to lag behind the collaborative requirements of each supply chain domain. A truly functional collaborative design will be leveraged if it is good enough, and there are many applications of collaboration across supply chain applications that simply have not been considered. This is why it is important that supply chain software vendors study the Arena Solutions authorization model.

Implementing the BMMS

As has been discussed up to this point, a good BMMS can improve so many areas that it should be one of the very highest upgrade priorities. A good BMMS is a bit like a very talented leader on a sports team: he or she makes all the other players (i.e., applications) better and more sustainable. Supply chain professionals often consider the BOM as simply a master data object that supports production and procurement. However, the BOM can be used as the basis for a project plan for new product procurement.

A BMMS tends to be less expensive than a number of systems that rely upon it, and it's perplexing as to why companies tend to underinvest in BMMS. Weak BOM maintenance capabilities negatively impact very expensive ERP system implementation projects, and a relatively small percentage of companies can really gain maximum leverage of their BOM data because they simply lack the software and the know-how. Many companies have wasted enormous sums of money implementing "PLM" systems purchased from the large monopoly vendors, but the only companies that seem to "get" the SaaS-based BMMS concept are smaller vendors. In fact, Arena Solutions doesn't even compete in the same space as SAP (although they do compete with Oracle since Oracle purchased Agile). Arena Solutions itself only has around twenty million dollars in yearly revenue and all they have done is create the best collaborative application of any supply chain application I have seen.

The ROI of a BMMS Implementation

BMMS's are simpler to implement and can be implemented far more quickly than many other systems that rely upon them. They are simpler and easier to use, which means user training and change management are far less effort. Therefore, lower costs, shorter implementation time horizon, and better payback are all features of a good SaaS-based BMMS.

The payback or return on investment on a BMMS must be viewed comprehensively; how does the BMMS improve all the systems that rely upon BOM information? The ROI of a BMMS must be measured by the improvements and cost reductions in the ERP system, in the external planning systems, and in design and engineering, along with improvements in collaboration both inside the implementing company and its supply chain partners. Furthermore, the ability to effectively archive and reuse old BOMs must also be included in the ROI.

Socializing the BMMS at the Company Performing the Implementation

In terms of the implementation, a lot of work must go into ensuring the BMMS can fully support all of the business requirements. This includes the following tasks:

1. The BOM and part association must be imported into the BMMS.

2. The part, external partner, and individuals (internal and external) must be collected and imported into the BMMS.

3. The users who will access the BMMS directly must be trained, and interfaces must be developed to those applications that will connect to the BMMS through file transfer.

4. All participants should be educated as to how the BMMS will work and how the company's current process will be supported and changed in order to enable the future state.

Gaining Access to a Demo BMMS

Anyone can become familiar with how a BMMS works by simply logging into Arena Solutions' online BMMS demo system. This demo environment has a sample data set, but contains the same functionality that one would see when Arena is live at one's own company.

Being able to log in to a demo system like this has great benefits for software selection decision-making, as the company can, with very little cost and effort, determine if the solution would be a good fit for their needs. Having such a demo version available for customers to test undermines the common strategy of many of the larger vendors, which is to keep their solution under wraps and control the ability of others to review the software. Many vendors limit those reviewing the software to just the executive decision makers, who only get to review the software in a controlled environment where a presales consultant walks them through a canned demo. Most enterprise software is sold without any of the people who will actually be using the software ever seeing it, much less getting to experiment with it. This situation is one of the rules, which I have coined "Sun Tzu for the marketing strategy enterprise software vendors," which is available at the link below:

http://www.scmfocus.com/enterprisesoftwarepolicy/2012/06/10/sun-tzu-for-enterprise-software-vendors/

Arena Solution's open and universally-available demo environment allows the company to gather opinions from a wide variety of groups, particularly from those that will be using the system the most, and for a vote to be taken as to whether solution A or B would be most valuable. An OEM can also ask suppliers and contract manufacturers to test-drive the demo to see if they would also be in favor of the system, as they will also need to use it in the end. In fact, when compared to traditional enterprise software selection (where the solution is kept under wraps and a small cadre of executive decision makers gets a short and highly-controlled demo), the direct access method provided by Arena seems entirely superior. Companies that expose their applications in this manner are showing confidence in the ability of their application to speak for itself. Test-driving the application allows users to have a say in the systems they will be using, rather than having systems they would have never selected dropped into their laps and being told by executives to "make it work." In fact, the level of input the user community has to the software selection process is a major determining factor of a software implementation's success.

When I first logged into Arena years ago, I recall immediately feeling comfortable using the application. I looked forward to using it, and developed a screen scrapping service, which pulled data from Arena and published it to a separate web page. It was all very easy. Compared with much of the software I use (particularly SAP, where it takes years to become proficient with the application and there always seems to be some new hidden functionality or problem looming in on the horizon), playing in the Arena Solutions environment was remarkably refreshing.

Conclusion

Obtaining a quality BMMS is central to the strategy of BOM management as described in this book. A good BMMS creates positive externalities that improve the use of all of the systems that rely upon BOM information. It is also an application that allows a company to do things such as efficient BOM archival, sophisticated BOM search and relationship retrieval, and supplier and contract manufacturer management, as well as integrate the design and engineering and the supply chain parts of the company. Furthermore, a good BMMS eliminates the need for time-wasting discussions of whether to store the BOM in one fashion or another. A good BMMS can effortlessly present the BOM in the multiple ways required by different departments, and the fact that it can do this makes the BMMS an effective shared system, allowing it to be a single repository and single source of truth for BOM information.

The part is the central grouping mechanism within a BMMS. The BMMS allows a high degree of control over who can view each part. A good BMMS has a very capable associative functionality, as well as a nuanced authorization or permissions model that allows the different actors to control the parts that they have been given access to view or change, and keeps the rest of the parts database hidden from their view. Being able to control access allows a company to provide access to, and obtain input from, a very large supplier base without compromising the privacy or intellectual property of the OEM or implementing company, or of the suppliers and contract manufacturers; the suppliers and manufacturers cannot see one another's inputs to the BMMS. Because the notes and communications are retained and archived within the BMMS, a BMMS is actually a type of group-ware. A good BMMS not only improves the internal efficiency of the company in all aspects related to the BOM, it also—and quite effectively—lowers the cost of doing business with the company for supply chain partners.

Costing and cost management is greatly enhanced with a BMMS. Costing can be seen within the BMMS at the subcomponent or subassembly level, or for the entire BOM. Companies that have a good BMMS can understand their potential costs better that those that do not have a BMMS, and they can also develop a more information-rich supplier or vendor (or contract manufacturer) list, which can be leveraged between all present and future BOMs. The BMMS also allows prototype component costs to be tracked separately from production costs, allowing the company to obtain a more accurate estimate of actual costs. Furthermore, because a BMMS can be so easily queried, estimates can be derived from the BMMS without even sending out requests for quotations, meaning that the company can better allocate its limited analytical time between various potential products.

The BMMS can represent deeply-nested BOMs very easily. This is the preferred way for some engineers to see and interact with the BOM, as nested subassemblies can be leveraged across different BOMs. However, other engineers may prefer to see the BOM without its hierarchy. A good BMMS can accommodate both of these engineers. Multi-level BOMs are also important for complex and/or configurable products so that, for example, change orders can be made to only address subsets of levels within the BOM. A multi-level BOM also allows a company to share only the subassembly design with their supply chain partner. Because the levels and the subassemblies are a form of grouping, the maintainability of this data is improved. Multi-level BOMs with subassemblies also allow for easier internal organization, which supports the ability for higher-risk subassemblies to be identified and tracked by design and engineering.

A BMMS can never work properly if it can only present the BOM in one way, as is the case with ERP systems or planning systems. So many groups rely upon the BOM but have such different needs in terms of how the BOM information is presented. However, a well designed BMMS can easily support these diverse groups and diverse needs by presenting the BOM information in the way that each group wants to see it, and by providing each group with their own customized way of dealing with BOM information. Not having to fight over how BOM information is presented can greatly reduce conflict and increase cooperation between groups, both inside and outside of the company.

BMMS software design needs to be based on the BOM management requirements that have been described in this chapter. Too many companies purchase PLM solutions that are simply cobbled together from existing functionality in ERP systems. Paradoxically, at least in some cases, these "solutions" are not even effective at elementary BOM management and cannot allow a company to do the majority of things listed in this book. There are few really effective solutions in the BOM management space, and to be frank, several vendors are offering their clients vaporware in a slick marketing wrapper. After reading this book, I suspect it will be a little more difficult for companies to pull the wool over the eyes of as many executive decision makers. Adjusting pre-existing software that had a different initial purpose is not going to work very well, and will not lead to the benefits that I have described in this chapter and in this book.

While the official definition of a BOM is the listing *"...of raw material, sub-assemblies, intermediate assemblies, sub-components, components, parts and the quantities of each,"* BMMS systems combine many other types information to provide multi-dimensional abilities with the BOM. A BMMS includes design drawings, approved vendor lists, and many other related data that were mentioned earlier in this chapter to enable a much higher degree of control over the BOM management process. Searching for things tediously across many systems and many file folders can be done by querying just one system, organizing the information much better. This is highlighted by the quote below from Arena Solutions:

> *For each part on your master list you should know who the acceptable manufacturers are as well as which vendors sell those parts. Having a single approved source for a given part will prevent people from guessing and ordering the wrong components.*
>
> *Most companies like to reuse parts from current products when they develop new products as a way to both purchase in larger volumes and reduce engineering and manufacturing risks. But when products are designed by different teams, commonalities can be missed.*
> — "Beyond Colored Folders and Spreadsheets: Next-Generation Document
> Control for the Medical Device Industry," Arena Solutions 2011

A well-designed BMMS is as much a content management system (although a very customized form of content management when compared to a solution such as Drupal) as it is groupware as it is also supplier collaboration software. That is, the BMMS could be classified as several different categories of software, a quality that relates to the next point.

A good BMMS makes it easy to get data into the application. The data that supports the BMMS comes from many sources. Arena Solutions imports data through its import templates, which have mapping and error checking capabilities. Arena

Solutions also allows for the common PDX format to be imported, which is supported by the iNEMI standard accepted in the manufacturing industry. Furthermore, Arena also offers a free PDX viewer so those that do not have access to the Arena Solutions BMMS can access this data.

The terminology of "product lifecycle management" or PLM, and its adoption by many companies that offer BMMS applications, has been a major error and major impediment to the understanding and adoption of these systems. PLM is not, and can never be, a single application and there is no logic for continuing the use of PLM to describe any product. I am continually explaining the difference between a PLM offering and the functionality of a BMMS. A term that is illogical, that must be continually explained year after year, and which can trick executives into making poor software selections, is not a good term and should be abandoned. However, I don't expect this to happen because by using the term PLM, vendors who lack real BMMS functionality can pretend that they do. The term confuses most people, but some software vendors and consultants are actually in the business of confusing their clients. The less competitive a vendor's software is, the more ethereal and ill-defined it needs to be. Look no further than the MDM (master data management) software category for more evidence of this rule of thumb. To cut through the marketing hyperbole, this chapter has listed the questions to ask of any BMMS solution. The answers to just these questions can dramatically improve the abilities of companies to select the right BMMS solution.

The BOM is a beehive of changes, particularly when it is in the design stage. However, many of these changes are only relevant to one particular group that uses the system. For instance, the many changes that occur to a BOM prior to the BOM being released to production are not of interest to the groups concerned with supply chain planning. When a BOM is released to production, much of the information will not be ported to the MRP or planning system because it is unnecessary and there is nowhere to place this data— these systems only have a limited set of fields that hold BOM information. Third, the fields that are used by the different groups that rely upon BOM information greatly change depending upon the group in question. A good BMMS is able to maintain and archive all the information related to the BOM without exposing information to specific individuals and groups that do not need to or want to see it. In a good BMMS, not every person in every group is assigned to every part and subcomponent. This filtering allows users to see only what they need to see and keeps the user from being overwhelmed with information that is not of interest to them. Finally, there are many revisions to BOMs that are not yet in production, may never be produced, or are no longer produced, but which are still held and archived in the BMMS. This library of BOMs enhances the company's knowledge of its own products and greatly increases BOM reuse. Arena Solutions is so effective at maintaining this information that one of the improvements brought by their systems is greatly reduced cost and improved efficiency in BOM archival.

Of all the supply chain applications I have worked with, the BMMS has the highest collaborative requirements, and Arena Solutions has developed the most effective collaborative application of any enterprise vendor that I have seen. The supplier collaboration applications in the supply chain space have received most of the press, but the functionality and even the design concept of these applications greatly lags behind what Arena Solutions has developed, even though Arena is still a relatively small company (something I see changing in the future). Also, many people do not associate collaboration with BOM management solutions.

In this chapter, a good deal of time was spent describing Arena Solutions' authorization or permissions model. A BMMS must have a very capable authorization model because without one, companies will end up revealing information they do not want revealed to people inside and outside the company. The Arena Solutions' authorization model is another example of a best practice in software design, and I have not seen a comparable model in any other software. SAP's authorization model, about which several books have been written, appears to be from a different era when compared to Arena. Arena's authorization model is easy to administer, which is as important as its effectiveness in controlling access. Effective and efficient authorization models are extremely important to many classifications of software. Effective authorization control was always considered a strength of UNIX, and is one of the reasons it developed a strong reputation for security. Effective authorization has also been a major strength of the more recent releases of Apple OS X operating system.

Once a BMMS is populated with supporting data, it becomes a natural application to share outside as well as inside the company. The extra-enterprise collaboration needs of BMMS applications make them natural fits with the SaaS model, and SaaS vendors have a history of making their applications more capable of collaboration. Vendors that offer on-premises applications and that "dabble" in web interfaces that open here and there whenever collaboration is absolutely necessary, significantly lag SaaS vendors in collaboration, and this is true in any application where collaboration is a large part of the business requirement. SaaS vendors also offer very low per seat pricing (allowing a company to start with just a few seats) and month-to-month commitment solutions. I have compared a number of BMMS/PLM solutions, and in my opinion the SaaS-based solutions are the logical choice for a BMMS.

While I have not performed a quantitative analysis myself, intuitively it is quite obvious that BMMS has a high ROI. BMMS solutions are relatively simple to implement (especially as compared to many other supply chain applications, and the price of Saas-based BMMS solutions is quite low, which means that less money is put out to perform the implementation. Furthermore, because a BMMS has the potential to improve the efficiency of every application that uses BOM information, the benefits of implementing a BMMS come from many different areas. Many of these "efficiency" gains tend to be underemphasized by companies in favor of more quantifiable improvements. Therefore, while I have never attempted to quantify the ROI of a BMMS implementation, factors like the one just mentioned would make it a tricky exercise. However, the benefits in just one area can justify a BMMS implementation.

It's very easy to get access to a BMMS demo system. Arena Solutions offers a thirty-day trial application that is populated with some easy-to-understand test data. I have tried to explain a BMMS to the best of my ability and have provided a large number of application screenshots, but there is no substitute for actually using a system first hand. There is no cost to use the demo and it's easy to learn to use the application, so there are few reasons for a company interested in better BOM management not to log in to the Arena demo.

Only a small fraction of the companies that could benefit from BOM management software have implemented it or plan to implement it. Many companies tend to become confused as to what BOM management software is versus product life-cycle management (PLM), and many have fallen victim to highly unfocused and cobbled together PLM solutions from the major vendors that are simply not able to do what I describe in this book. PLM is not just one application, but is instead a variety of different functionality distributed throughout multiple supply chain applications. Furthermore, PLM is not the same as BOM management. PLM functionality can be anywhere in an application that does something to modify the product in concert with its lifecycle. BOM management software happens to be extremely focused on the lifecycle of products and so, in a way could be said to be part of PLM, but the BMMS is its own distinct application. Effective BOM management enables production planning. However, very few companies have effective BOM management software and are partially disabling their company by using standard ERP functionality to manage the BOM. BOM management has functionality that is related to life-cycle management, but it is not "defined" by its PLM functionality any more than demand planning, supply planning or production planning is defined by its PLM functionality. PLM is instead a distributed functionality that all supply chain applications have.

CHAPTER 8

BMMS Software and Suppliers Versus Contract Manufacturer Management

An effective BMMS can manage any level of interaction between the suppliers and a company, whether the supplier is an ancillary supplier that only supplies a few small value parts or a full contract manufacturer. Outsourced manufacturing (one subcategory of outsourcing that can apply to no manufacturing activities such as information technology) and contract manufacturing have been very strong trends over the past few decades. Contract manufacturing can be seen as an extreme form of supplier collaboration. In a normal customer-supplier relationship, the product is handed off between the companies. But in contract manufacturing, the subcontractor in effect becomes a part of the company, and, from concept through to manufacturing, the process requires collaborative input from both the customer and the supplier as if they were one company. In contract manufacturing, the BMMS system becomes increasingly important to accomplishing the objectives of both companies. On the following page are several quotes from *Product Lifecycle Management* by Antti Saaksvori and Anselmi Immonen:

...PLM system capabilities include workflow, program management, and project control features that standardize, automate and speed up product management operations. Web based systems enable companies easily to connect their globally dispersed facilities with each other and with outside organizations such as supplier, partners, and even customers. A PLM system is a collaboration backbone allowing people throughout extended enterprises to work together more effectively.

They can also work more effectively with suppliers in handling bids and quotes, exchange critical product information more smoothly with manufacturing facilities, and allow service technicians and spare part sales reps to quickly access required engineering data in the field.

It should be understood that Saaksvori and Immonen use the term PLM not to represent a specific BMMS, but the overall concept of PLM. In my view, these quotations become more accurate when the term BMMS is exchanged for PLM because these characteristics all apply directly to a BMMS.

Contract manufacturing essentially changes the OEM into more of a general contractor, with the work being performed by the subcontractors. Contract manufacturing is its own detailed topic with its own subject matter experts who are specialists in such things as how to choose the best contract manufacturer (CM) under all possible circumstances. Many CMs have become so large that they dwarf the OEMs they do business with, and hence the selection of a CM that is not too big for the OEM and that can give the OEM priority is a frequent topic of discussion within the CM area. This goes beyond negotiating leverage, as the CM may have certain volume requirements that the OEM must meet in order for the CM to accept their business. In fact, what is interesting about the development of contract manufacturing (and a topic I don't often hear discussed by economists or anyone else for that matter) is how contract manufacturing somewhat levels the playing field with OEMs. While at one time we discussed the "economies of scale" (or the efficiencies that come with size) of the OEM, it is now common to discuss the economies of scale of the CM. CMs serve as aggregation entities, spreading the production of many companies over human resources, equipment and plants.

How much of the production process to outsource is a frequent topic of discussion within OEMs. The more OEMs outsource contract manufacturing, the more they seem to want to and the more they increase the scope of the CM's role. For instance, at one time the OEMs performed all design and engineering and left only the manufacturing to the CMs. However, OEMs are increasingly content to outsource design as well while maintaining control over brand management, marketing, and supply chain management. This is highlighted by a quote from Arena Solutions:

> *Since the late 1990s, outsourcing has become a way of life for*
> *electronics manufacturers. Most OEMs no longer consider*
> *manufacturing to be a core competency. Even in cases where some*
> *of this capability is retained in-house, there is an ongoing effort*
> *to evaluate more activities that can be offloaded to a contract*
> *manufacturer (CM). These CMs, whose role in the electronics industry*
> *was previously limited to assembling printed circuit boards, have*
> *transformed themselves into large scale manufacturing powerhouses.*
> *Modern CMs provide their customers with a one-stop shop solution,*
> *providing excellence not only in manufacturing, but also in materials*
> *management, design and test services, order fulfillment and logistics.*
> "Beyond BOM 101: Next Generation Bills of Material Management,"
> Arena Solutions, 2011

The OEM is completely reliant upon so many companies for so many aspects of product design and manufacturing, and coordinating with the OEM increases the organization and communication requirements at contract manufacturers. This is something that a quality BMMS can help enable.

What Drives Contract Manufacturing?
The book *Supply Chain Brutalization: The Handbook for Contract Manufacturing,* defines contract manufacturing as follows:

A contract manufacturer is an enterprise, company concern, or individual that provides a manufacturing service to another company. This can be at the component level, such as a machined piston for a Harley Davidson engine, pharmaceutical drug for Pfizer, on up through subsystems integration, such as a cockpit display for a Sikorsky helicopter, or a complete point of sale product, like a laptop PC.

It is not easy to determine when a supplier ends and a contract manufacturer begins, so I have included the following definition from Wikipedia to further illuminate the subject:

In a contract manufacturing business model, the hiring firm approaches the contract manufacturer with a design or formula. The contract manufacturer will quote the parts based on processes, labor, tooling, and material costs. Typically, a hiring firm will request quotes from multiple CMs. After the bidding process is complete, the hiring firm will select a source, and then, for the agreed-upon price, the CM acts as the hiring firm's factory, producing and shipping units of the design on behalf of the hiring firm.

Here the distinction becomes clearer. The CM is not simply selling a product to its customer, but is offering an outsourced manufacturing capacity. The company buying from the CM has a great deal of flexibility in terms of defining the specification that is then manufactured, which also implies a great deal of information sharing, much more than is necessary for a normal supplier relationship. (This is an important distinction and further along in this book we will see how the CM is set up differently in Arena Solutions than a supplier.)

Cost is the driving force behind a company's reliance on CMs, and the costs are quite significant. According to *Supply Chain Brutalization,*

The labor costs in emerging regions are so low, they warrant a look. If the OEM can reduce COGS by an additional 10 to 15 percent, that number goes right to the bottom line.

Some industry sources have attempted to minimize the importance of labor costs in their decision to use contract manufacturers by stating that the manufacturing labor costs of many products is, for example, only ten percent of the overall manufacturing costs. However, the argument is misleading, and perhaps even deliberately misleading. The percentage is so low because contract manufacturers are located in countries where labor costs are low. If the same product were made in a developed country, the labor cost percentage would greatly increase, which of course was the main motivating factor for using a contract manufacturer in a low-cost country in the first place. Some proponents of contract manufacturing want to have it both ways. They want to tell companies what great cost savings will result from contract manufacturing (much of them directly related to lower labor costs), then turn around and say labor costs are not a driver for outsourcing manufacturing. If labor costs were not a main driver for contract manufacturing, then the vast majority of CM factories would not be in countries where labor costs are low.

Contract Manufacturing by Industry

Contract manufacturing tends to be concentrated in several industries. According to Wikipedia, some of the most intensive users of contract manufacturing are the following:

- Aerospace
- Defense
- Computer
- Semiconductor
- Energy
- Medical
- Food manufacturing
- Personal care
- Pharmaceutical
- Automotive

The largest CMs are concentrated in high tech and in terms of geography the largest contract manufacturers are in Asia. Some CMs are well-known brands in their own right, such as Flextronics, Celestica and Sanmina-SCI. However, most CMs are not global brands, but they produce for very well-known companies. Many CMs produce competing products off of the same production line. The giant CM Foxconn employs roughly one million people, primarily in China, making them approximately half as large as Walmart in number of employees, even though their revenues were only fourteen of Walmart (China's currency is deliberately undervalued by the Chinese Government to promote exports, so a direct apples-to-apples comparison of revenue is difficult).

Bottom line, many of the best-known brands no longer do very much manufacturing; many prefer to follow the "Nike" model where all manufacturing is outsourced. Furthermore, the trend is rather consistent ever since it began. For instance, Nike began its life relying upon external manufacturing, and this was, in fact, the topic of Phil Knight's Master's thesis in graduate school. But now many companies that previously manufactured themselves and manufactured domestically have moved to either outsourced or contract manufacturing.

There are many implications of the growth of contract manufacturing, and they are not all positive when one looks beyond the benefits provided to individual companies through higher profits. Considering it's such a massive trend, the topic is covered sparingly in books. Two of the few books on the topic are *The Black Book of Outsourcing,* where contract manufacturing is treated as just one of many types of outsourced supplier relationships, and the amusingly titled *Supply Chain Brutalization: The Handbook for Contract Manufacturing,* which I quote several times in this book. One book that one may not find by searching for contract manufacturing is *Who Really Made Your Car?* which describes the high degree of contract manufacturing of subcomponents in the automotive industry. Both this book, as well as several other sources, estimate that only twenty-five percent to thirty percent of the average automobile's value is actually produced by the OEM (Toyota, GM, etc.).

Supply Chain Brutalization points out the following:

> *Automotive provides the volumes of consumer electronics, but contrary to the EMS ODM model of vertical integration, less than 25 percent of an automobile is manufactured by the maker. Components and subsystems, such as ignition systems, tail lights, interior liners, and power seats are all subcontracted to third parties, rendering the car maker to be a chassis manufacturer and systems integrator so to speak.*

The book *Who Really Made Your Car?* further proposes that one of the major reasons for the rise of Toyota is not only its internal manufacturing processes, which are of course highly touted, but Toyota's ability to serve as a system integrator by developing highly collaborative relationships with the many contract manufacturers and suppliers that make the majority of Toyota's automobiles (with Toyota primarily performing the function of final assembly).

There are many labor, income inequality and environmental issues (pollution in countries with little regulation, as well as the energy and carbon footprint for transporting manufacturing items such great distances). It's a complex topic, which covers many areas. The complexity extends to whether using CMs is even beneficial for the OEMs that use them, at least in the long term, as this quote from *Supply Chain Brutalization,* explains:

> *The lines of demarcation are vanishing. Contractually, the traditional CM was the carpenter in the relationship—not the architect. The liabilities were clear: the performance of the product was never guaranteed, just the workmanship. Now the ODM (Original Design Manufacturer) changes all of that by taking on product development and post sales support. Leaving just the marketing to the OEM.*
>
> *The ODM trend has brought the contract manufacturing full circle—from breaking the vertical integration model at the OEM, to reinventing it in a purchased commodity. Originally, we outsourced*

the assembly content to a CM whose costs were lower because they had no product marketing or product development. That was the sales pitch for the CM.

Now especially in Asia, the contract manufacturers are revering the model to bolster the bottom line. First, engineering services are offered, then tooled parts such as plastics and metal are added. Finally, reference designs are offered—PC motherboards, for example. This offering can eliminate design cycle times and costs for their OEM customers.

The question is on the table: If an ODM that specializes in products (like a notebook PC) does everything for the OEM except the marketing function, at what point does the ODM take the last step and jump into the game, boosting those single digit margins to true OEM margins?

Clearly, contract manufacturers can gain the ability to compete with the OEMs that originally hired them. The PC portion of the business for US brands such as HP, which relied heavily on CMs for enhancing their profits, is in decline, and previously unknown consumer brands that started as CMs (such as ASUS) have become OEMs, effectively cutting out OEMs in the US. It should be understood that the motivations for CMs to become OEMs is enormous. The profitability of CMs is so low, and OEMs negotiate so aggressively against them, that the desire of most CMs must naturally be to become OEMs. The CMs that are large and capable are currently moving in this direction or have already accomplished their goal. Note the quotation below regarding ASUS's (Asustek's) future plans:

Taiwanese Asustek Computer Inc. plans to split its operations of branding and EMS operations. The split was earlier planned to be done in 2008; however, the turbulence in the EMS sector at the moment has pushed Asustek to proceed with the split as soon as possible...Asustek plans to concentrate on branding business while creating a new EMS company. The Asustek move is aimed at challenging the status of Foxconn's No.1 position in the EMS sector.

— Supply Chain Brutalization

Contract Manufacturing Implications on BOM Management

CMs are an important force in manufacturing, and are driving the need for more interactive BOM software and for cross-company collaboration. Contract manufacturers have a challenge with respect to sharing information with the OEM, as described in the quote below:

Contract manufacturers receive data in variable formats from multiple customers and formalize it into a common format for processing. When change occurs, the change notice (internal document) is routed throughout the enterprise and has an impact analysis done by all applicable disciplines. The impact can entail: billable rework for work in progress, modifications to test equipment and other tooling, costs and lead time changes resultant from new components, billable obsolete inventory for components removed, or, billable scrap. A formal response is routed back to the customer and the changes are approved or disapproved.

— Supply Chain Brutalization

However, a BMMS helps structure this information, making an OEM more appealing to work with and lowering the amount of work required for both the OEM and the CM.

With contracting manufacturing, the need for better functionality of BOM management software has increased in the following ways:

1. Many more individuals and companies must interact with the BOM.

2. With contract manufacturing, there are many more issues with respect to intellectual property protection. A contract manufacturing relationship means that the details of design and manufacture are shared between the OEM and the CM.

3. The BOM becomes a central collaborative object among various companies.

4. Interaction with the BOM is now much more greatly distributed across geography.

5. The need for security, role control and authorization is much more pronounced than in the past.

6. The overall complexity of supplier management is increasing. To manage contract manufacturers and suppliers effectively, the system must have a high administration efficiency level.

Arena Solutions brings this point up in the following quotation:

> *Outsourced manufacturing is undertaken to reduce costs for things such as labor and parts. However, outsourcing requires that design documentation be rigorous and accurate; excellent product documentation results in better product quality and lowered maintenance costs. The process of handing off documentation to an outside party introduces a kind of formality to the process that raises the bar for the quality of the engineering deliverable. But this greatly increases the pressure on the engineering group to positively document every aspect of the product.*
>
> *OEMs often need to collect competitive quotes from multiple contract manufacturers during the sourcing process. Traditionally, this procedure involves producing duplicate copies of full product documentation, followed by a bidding phase where detailed quote information is gathered. In the meantime, if any part specifications change, the updated information must be packaged and re-sent to each manufacturer. With Arena, there is a single instance of the product data available online and always up to date.*
>
> — "The Arena Solutions Guide to Outsourcing: Removing Barriers, Maintaining Boundaries," Arena Solutions, 2011

Arena Solutions and Contract Manufacturing

Arena is used to connect OEMs to contract manufacturers, and Arena Solutions is frequently used in the high tech industry. In addition to their BMMS product, Arena Solutions also makes a product called the Parts List. Parts list is integrated with a number of major electronic distributor websites. I see Arena's BMMS as truly a cross-industry product; however, as the high tech industry is one of the most intensively outsourced of all manufacturing industries, it is natural that Arena would be popular in this industry.

Converting Between a Typical Supplier and a Contract Manufacturer

Essentially, the contract manufacturer is the very upper end of suppliers. They provide more services than other suppliers and they also provide more information to the BMMS and require access to more information from the BMMS. Information requirements are all established in the administration of the BMMS.

I will now go through the process of making a normal supplier into a contract manufacturer.

As you can see, I currently have no suppliers assigned to this workspace.

User Account Information   Cancel

Click **Create Account** to establish your free Arena user account.

* denotes a required field

User Information

* First Name	Tom
* Last Name	Snapp
* Title	CEO
* Telephone Number	4084900242
Skype Name	

Arena works with Skype software to enable real-time voice and chat communication for Arena users.

User Login
Create the password that you will use for your new Arena account. Be sure to remember the password you select, as you will need it every time you wish to log in. (For security purposes, the account activation confirmation email you receive from us will not include your password.)

* Email Address	**scmfocus@gmail.com**
* Password	••••••••

Passwords must be 6-18 characters in length and contain at least one letter and one number.

* Re-enter Password	••••••••

Please verify that you have correctly entered your new password.

Company Information

* Company Name	Super GPS
* Street Address	1212 Mountain Street
* City	Campbell
* State	California
* Postal/Zip Code	95008
* Country	US
* Website	www.scmfocus.com
* Industry	- Select - Aerospace & Defense Automotive Consumer Products High Tech & Electronics

Please select all that apply

* Number of Employees	11 - 50
* Annual Revenue	Under $5M

To use this registration form, your browser must be configured to accept cookies.

Create Account ►

However, I can add a new supplier to the workspace.

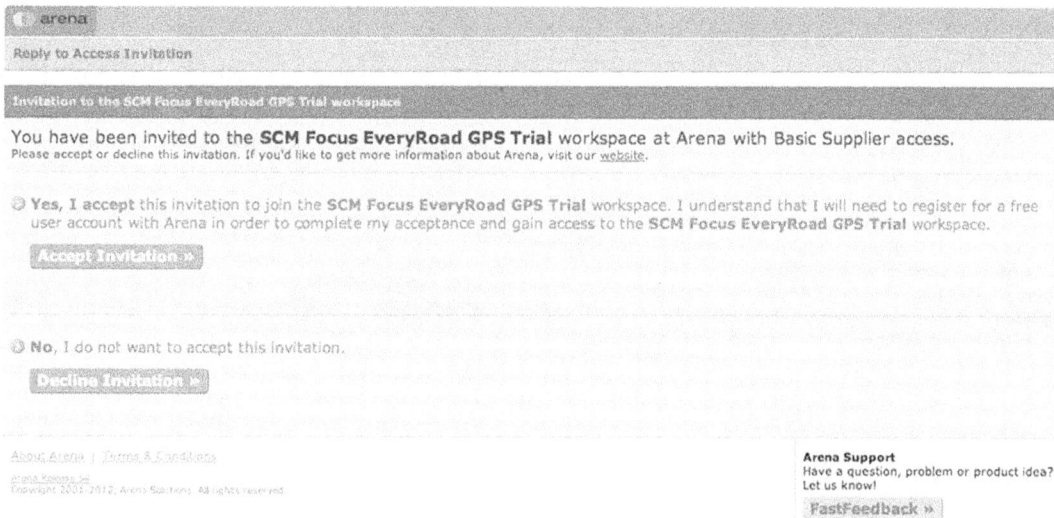

When this is done, a confirmation email is sent to the supplier, and the supplier can choose whether to accept or reject the invitation.

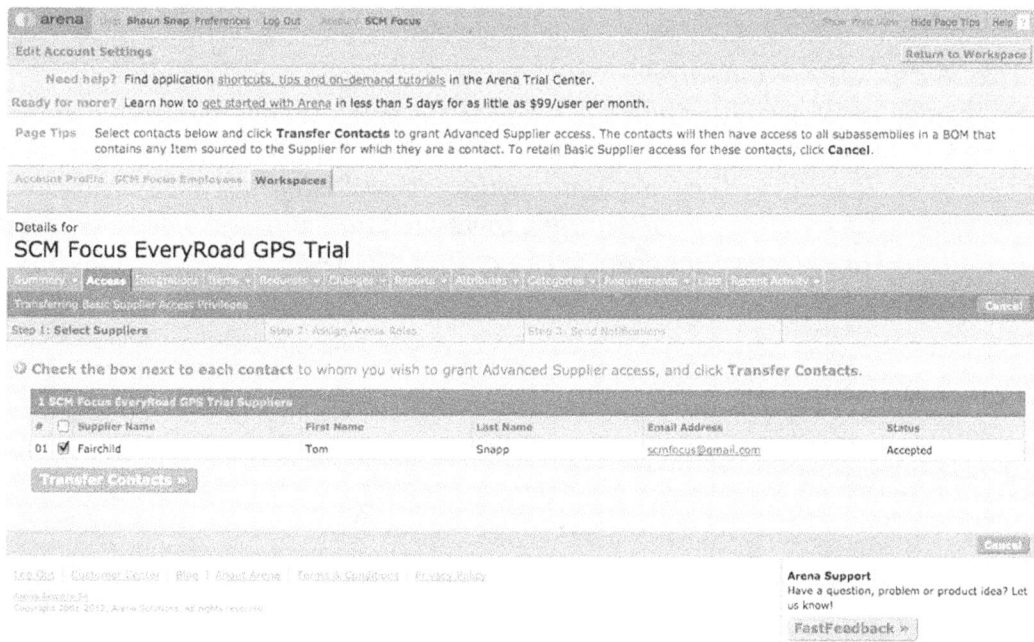

Now that the supplier is created, we can move to the next step of converting it to a contract manufacturer.

The role that is assigned is extremely important. The highest authorization level for a supplier can be set for a contract manufacturer. As you can see, I am selecting "Read-Write Contract Manufacturer (File Upload, Quoting)." However, another contract manufacturer may only be at "Read-Only Contract Manufacturer (Cost Visibility)." This illustrates the fact that even with contract manufacturers, there are many different types. More detail on what the role in the screen shot can do can be found by selecting "Access Roles" underneath "Access."

arena User Shaun Snap Preferences Log Out Account: SCM Focus   Show Print View Hide Page Tips Help

Edit Account Settings   Return to Workspace

Need help? Find application shortcuts, tips and on-demand tutorials in the Arena Trial Center.

Ready for more? Learn how to get started with Arena in less than 5 days for as little as $99/user per month.

Page Tips   This is the Access view in the Account Administration tool, showing the Access Roles subview. Each user's access to a workspace is defined by a role in one of four categories: Employee (users with access to all objects in the workspace), Partner (users from outside your account with access to all objects in the workspace), Basic Supplier (users from outside your account with access to Items sourced to them) and Advanced Supplier (users from outside your account with access to Items sourced to them and those Items' first-level BOMs). Roles include world settings that specify the types of objects a user can access and the object-level functions that can be performed. Roles also include access privileges, which use data filters to define access to specific sets of objects and permissions to indicate the views and subviews that can be seen and edited for those objects as well as the commands that can be performed on them. Click any role name to see its settings and privileges, and use the **View Privilege Details** link to see filter and permission details. Click any question mark icon for more information about a given section.

Account Profile   SCM Focus Employees   **Workspaces**

Details for
SCM Focus EveryRoad GPS Trial

Summary ▾ **Access** Integrations Items ▾ Requests ▾ Changes ▾ Reports ▾ Attributes ▾ Categories ▾ Requirements ▾ Lists Recent Activity ▾

Users **Access Roles**

Employee Roles
These roles give users in your account access to all workspace objects.

P I R C S SI F Rp Ro
▶ **Approver Employee [Read-Only, No Cost Visibility]**
Grants read-only access privileges for all Workspace objects (with Costing information hidden) and participation privileges for Changes and Requests

P I R C S SI F Rp Ro
▶ **Approver Employee [Read-Only]**
Grants read-only access privileges for all Workspace objects and participation privileges for Changes and Requests

P R I R C C S SI F Rp Ro
▶ **Full Employee [Design Revision Creation]**
Grants creation, participation and read-write access privileges for all Workspace objects (and includes Design Stage Item Revision release privileges)

P R I R C C S SI F Rp Ro
▶ **Full Employee [No Revision Creation, Buyer]**
Grants creation, participation and select read-write access privileges (for managing Sourcing and Costing data) for all Workspace objects (but does not include Item Revision release privileges)

P R I R C C S SI F Rp Ro
▶ **Full Employee [No Revision Creation, No Cost Visibility]**
Grants creation, participation and read-write access privileges for all Workspace objects (but hides Costing information and does not include Item Revision release privileges)

P R I R C C S SI F Rp Ro
▶ **Full Employee [No Revision Creation]**
Grants creation, participation and read-write access privileges for all Workspace objects (but does not include Item Revision release privileges)

Here is a full employee role below:

▼Full Employee [Design Revision Creation]

View Privilege Details

Grants creation, participation and read-write access privileges for all Workspace objects (and includes Design Stage Item Revision release privileges)

World Settings ?

Show Object	Create	Import	Export
✓ Projects	✓		
✓ Items	✓	✓	✓
✓ Requests	✓		
✓ Changes	✓		
✓ Suppliers	✓	✓	✓
✓ Supplier Items	✓	✓	✓
✓ Files	✓	✓	✓
✓ Reports	✓		

Note:
While settings and privileges for all application objects are shown here, individual Workspace access is defined only by the settings and privileges that reference features enabled in a user's Workspace.

11 Access Privileges

- Read-Only Access for all Projects
- Project Manager Access for Managed Projects
- Read-Write Access and Design Stage Revision Release Privileges for all Items
- Read-Write Access for all Requests
- Read-Write Access for all Changes
- Withdraw Privileges for Own Change Submissions
- Read-Write Access for all Suppliers
- Read-Write Access for all Supplier Items
- Read-Write Access for all Files
- Read-Only Access for all Shared Reports
- Read-Write Access for Own Personal Reports

Here is how that compares to a Read-Write Contract Manufacturing Role:

▼Read-Write Contract Manufacturer [File Upload, Quoting]

View Privilege Details

Grants limited read-write access privileges (File upload and Costing data entry) for sourced Items, Items in their first-level BOMs and related Suppliers and Supplier Items

World Settings ?

Show Object	Create	Import	Export
✘ Projects	✘		
✓ Items	✘	✘	✓
~ Requests	~		
✓ Changes	✘		
✓ Suppliers	✘	✘	✓
✓ Supplier Items	✘	✘	✓
✘ Files	✓	✘	✓
✘ Reports	✘		

Note:
While settings and privileges for all application objects are shown here, individual Workspace access is defined only by the settings and privileges that reference features enabled in a user's Workspace.

Note:
Supplier Access to the Requests World is managed in the Supplier Access Subview of the Requests View.

8 Access Privileges

- Quoting, File Upload Access for Sourced Items (and Related Suppliers and Supplier Items)
- Quoting, File Upload Access for First-Level Child Items of Sourced Items (and Related Suppliers and Supplier Items)
- Editing Privileges for Supplier-Created Requests
- Submission Privileges for Supplier-Created Requests
- Supplier Participation Privileges for Requests
- Read-Only Supplier Access for Shared Changes
- Supplier Participation Privileges for Shared Changes
- Supplier Implementation Privileges for Shared Changes

Here is how that compares to a Read-Only Contract Manufacturing Role:

▾Read-Only Contract Manufacturer [Cost Visibility]   View Privilege Details

Grants limited read-only access privileges for sourced Items, Items in their first-level BOMs and related Suppliers and Supplier Items

World Settings 7					7 Access Privileges
Show	Object	Create	Import	Export	
✕	Projects	✕			Read-Only Access for Sourced Items (and Related Suppliers and Supplier Items)
✓	Items	✕	✕	✓	Read-Only Access for First-Level Child Items of Sourced Items (and Related Suppliers and Supplier Items)
	Requests				
✓	Changes	✕			Editing Privileges for Supplier-Created Requests
✓	Suppliers	✕	✕	✓	Submission Privileges for Supplier-Created Requests
✓	Supplier Items	✕	✕	✓	
✕	Files	✕	✕	✓	Supplier Participation Privileges for Requests
✕	Reports	✕			Read-Only Supplier Access for Shared Changes

Note:
While settings and privileges for all application objects are shown here, individual Workspace access is defined only by the settings and privileges that reference features enabled in a user's Workspace.

Supplier Participation Privileges for Shared Changes

Note:
Supplier Access to the Requests World is managed in the Supplier Access Subview of the Requests View.

Now we will go back to the conversion to contract manufacturer workflow.

Details for
SCM Focus EveryRoad GPS Trial

| Summary ▾ | Access | Integrations | Items ▾ | Requests ▾ | Changes ▾ | Reports ▾ | Attributes ▾ | Categories ▾ | Requirements ▾ | Lists | Recent Activity ▾ |

Transferring Basic Supplier Access Privileges   « Back   Cancel

| Step 1: Select Suppliers | Step 2: Assign Access Roles | Step 3: **Send Notifications** | |

To complete this process without notifying the affected users, click **Transfer Without Notification**. You will be responsible for informing these users that their access privileges have changed.

Transfer Without Notification »

To complete this process and send a notification email to each affected user, review the email below and add your comments in the Message text box. When finished, click **Transfer With Notification**.

This email will be sent to the transferred contacts:

From	**Shaun Snap <proxy-mailer@arenasolutions.com>**
Email Text	Dear <Recipient>

Shaun Snap has granted you Advanced Supplier access in the SCM Focus EveryRoad GPS Trial workspace at Arena. The next time you log in to the Arena application, you will be able to see not only the Items for which you are a designated Supplier, but also the Items included in those Items' BOMs.

This type of access gives you greater visibility into the SCM Focus EveryRoad GPS Trial workspace. If you have any questions about this change in access, please contact Shaun Snap at ultra.snapp@gmail.com.

Thank you for using Arena.

This additional message will be included in the email:

| Message | You are now a full contract manufacturer with all the system privileges that entails. | |

Transfer With Notification »

Notice the text that describes what has occurred.

Now we can see that an advanced supplier has been added to the workspace.

Hopefully these screenshots demonstrated how easy it is to manage suppliers or contract manufacturers if you have the right BMMS. Suppliers and contract manufacturers can be set up simply and quickly, and because of Arena's authorization level, they can be given only the access to the parts of the BOM database that they need to see, while keeping the rest of the information private.

The Standard Production Planning Process

Supply planning and production planning systems are designed to schedule a finished good, which has a BOM that is connected to various subcomponents and raw materials. These items are then procured in the right time and quantity required to support production of the finished good. The production process has two important components:

1. The bill of material is exploded in one location.

2. The production takes place in one location.

This is the simplest type of production. One can allow a single supply planning method to cascade through the BOM at a single location (if one is producing with make to stock; if one is planning with make assemble to order, then the components and subcomponents are kept in stock, but the finished good or component level is not). Now that we have outlined the process flow for the standard production planning process, we can move to the superplant concept and design.

The Superplant Concept

A superplant design is essentially the division of the various production steps into different locations. The overall BOM becomes a "modular" BOM, with parts of the BOM made in different locations. A company may use several factories, which may be close to each other or which may be in different countries, to perform different steps of the manufacturing process for different subcomponents. The difference is that stock transport orders are used to receive the subcomponents into the plant that performs final assembly rather than purchasing orders, making for a much more complicated supply planning design. Several important issues arise because of this design:

1. How should the stock transports be controlled between the factories? Stock transports may be designed to differ based upon whether or not the plants are within close proximity to one another. This topic is described in detail in this article: http://www.scmfocus.com/sapplanning/2012/07/24/synchronizing-integrated-factories-with-stock-transfers/

2. Stock transport requisitions (the precursor to STOs) are treated differently by SAP APO than purchase requisitions (the precursor to POs). For instance, the creation of purchase requisitions is part of the initial supply plan, while the stock transport requisition is an output of the deployment plan. A purchase requisition for a component can include purchase requisitions that are created for the component's subcomponents as well. However, a stock transport requisition is designed to request a transfer of a component from a different internal facility. If a component is managed internally, the component's production capacity is often much easier to model (companies that successfully model their supplier capacity are still relatively rare, although a PPM can be created in a vendor location in APO, so it is technically possible). However, interesting questions arise with respect to how

the procedure—let's say CTM—drives the demand through the various plants. The graphic below shows how transferring subcomponents between internal locations is different than producing a product in a single location exclusively with purchase requisitions.

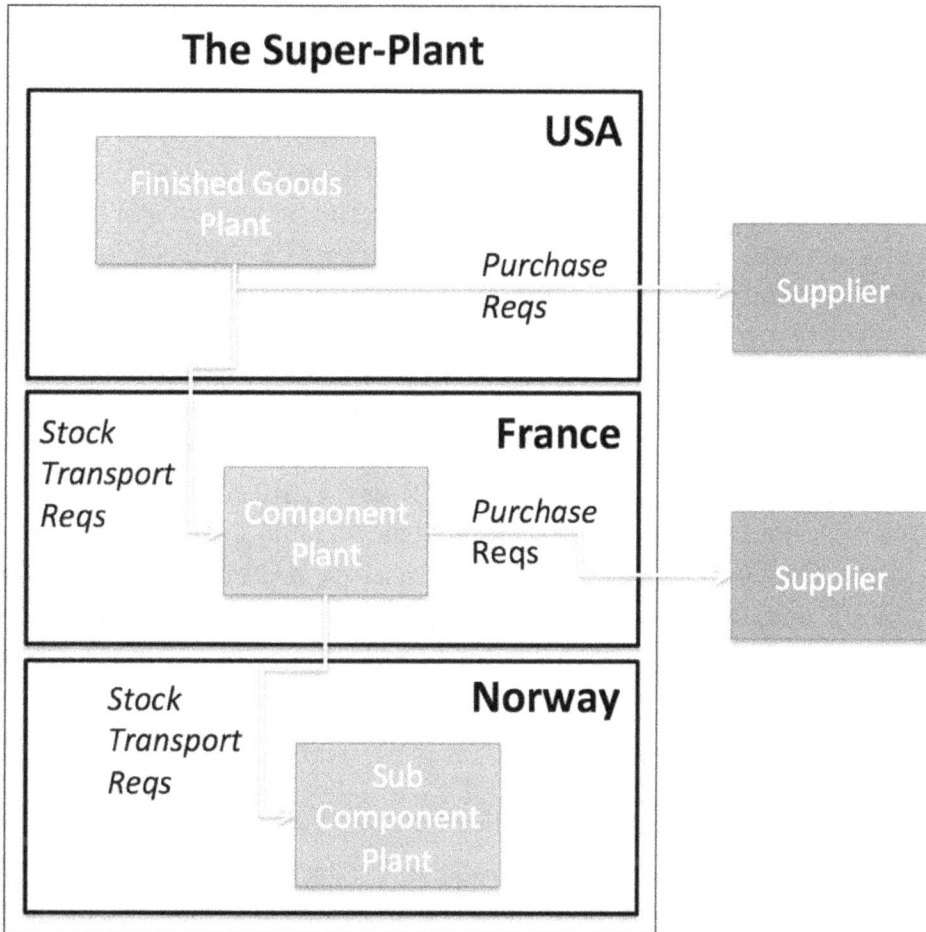

The Super-Plant

USA

Finished Goods Plant

Purchase Reqs → Supplier

Stock Transport Reqs

France

Component Plant

Purchase Reqs → Supplier

Stock Transport Reqs

Norway

Sub Component Plant

Essentially, the dependent demand that *"waterflows"* cleanly through the bill of materials when production is performed in a single location, is broken up into subunits or sub-bills of materials as the stock transfer requisitions are passed among various locations. It also means that the bill of materials is aggregated at the final assembly location, and the real bill of material is a composite made up of "miniature" bills of materials distributed in the different locations. Although tangential, this is a fractured and distributed bill of materials, and quite a bit different from the bill of materials that was developed and used by engineering and design when creating the product. This is an excellent example of how the bill of materials differs within a company depending upon the group using it, and shows again why the ERP system should never be the system of record of the bill of materials.

The Superplant Versus the Common Manufacturing Trend

Most companies are moving in the opposite direction of integrated factories with increased outsourcing of subcomponents and with the OEMs essentially taking the role of a general contractor. This is, of course, the contract manufacturing model that I spoke of earlier, with companies like Apple doing no production, and contract manufacturers making between two percent and three percent margins on cost structures based in the lowest cost countries (although it remains to be seen how long these companies can operate this model without becoming displaced either by retailers or CMs that create their own brand as ASUS has done). However, for companies that are still vertically integrated— where the plants that provide the components are subcomponents for a finished good—the concept of a superplant is quite useful in creating a mental model for how the production and supply planning process needs to be designed in the associated planning systems. There are several important differences between a standard production design and the superplant.

1. In a superplant, the bill of material is distributed in multiple locations.

2. The production takes place in multiple locations in a superplant.

3. Synchronizing the continuous material flow among factories is critical to maintaining production efficiencies. The triggering of stock transports may change depending upon plant proximity. In close proximity plants, the supply planning system may not need to be involved. http://www.scmfocus.com/sapplanning/2012/07/24/synchronizing-integrated- factories-with-stock-transfers/

4. In a macro sense at least, each factory can be thought of as a work center, and the flow through the supply network, for internal locations at least, can be considered a routing.

5. Because the production is distributed across factories, the overall manufacturing process cannot be capacity-constrained using a single bottleneck resource on a "single global production line." In effect, each production line in each factory is separately constrained.

6. An important consideration with the superplant design is the prioritization of internal over external demand. This means using both constraint-based planning in addition to being able to automatically prioritize the by-demand type. This is a very good fit with the capabilities of a prioritization based supply planning method like SAP APO CTM, and would mean that CTM would be set up to control all the product locations where the finished good, the components, and the subcomponents are planned in the supply network.

Conclusion

An effective BMMS allows for the efficient management of various levels of interaction between suppliers and contract manufacturers. Controlling the views and access of outside parties is a very good test of an application's authorization model. A good BMMS allows not only for suppliers and contract manufacturers to have better information as input to the bids they provide back to the owner of the BMMS, but also allows the owner of the BMMS to better manage their supplier and contract manufacturer information. The ability to manage this information may include having a better handle on the pricing of various components from different suppliers, as well as other aspects that can help the BMMS owner make the best purchasing decision.

Contract manufacturing has been a major area of growth for specific manufacturing industries and requires even more integration between the OEM and the CM. It is not at all surprising that Arena Solutions has been successful in selling to companies that need to manage CMs. Contract manufacturing is a complex topic and is not very well documented, and while I have touched on some of the broader aspects of contract manufacturing, the main impact of contract manufacturing is that it increases the need for sophisticated BMMS software. Those software vendors that have developed their product to meet the challenging requirements of this market will have an advantage over those vendors that have not done so. Increasingly, the effectiveness of OEMs is measured not so much by their own manufacturing capabilities as much as how good a job they do at performing the role of general contractor, managing a wide network of subcontractors that perform most of the manufacturing, and increasingly, doing the design work as well. To excel in this new role, companies require the systems that allow them to meet these higher requirements for collaboration. Unfortunately, while companies have moved toward increased outsourcing of manufacturing, many of the supply chain systems that these same companies buy have not kept up, and not been made appreciably more collaborative. In this regard, younger companies such as Arena Solutions have an advantage over older companies as they had no older internally-oriented design to defend when they were developing their solution.

Those that have experience in contract manufacturing know that engaging in contract manufacturing increases the need for documentation management and document formality. A lower degree of organization and less rigorous technical documentation may be less detrimental when the documents are shared internally, and when many of the creators and consumers of such documentation may know each other. However, when documentation leaves the internal confines of the company and is shared across different countries with different languages and cultures, more standardization and consistency is required. While a BMMS cannot create better documentation, it does help organize the documentation, and make it more searchable and easier to find through its association with the precise part it describes. A BMMS also controls the versions of documents, so that suppliers and contract manufacturers work from the most up-to-date specifications and information. Document control increases quality, reduces the cost of interacting with suppliers, and reduces the cost of new product introductions overall. It can also reduce timelines, as there is far less rework.

A good BMMS allows easy and simple addition of suppliers and contract manufacturers to the system, as was demonstrated with screenshots in this chapter. This helps reduce the costs of dealing with supply chain partners, allowing more suppliers to be added to the BMMS database more easily.

A company's inability to manage a large supplier database shifts more power to the suppliers that have already gone through the approval process. This problem is much larger than BOM management and extends into my field of IT consulting work, where large consulting companies become preferred vendors, and promptly abuse this privilege by reducing the value they deliver and increasing their costs. In fact, many suppliers of goods and services in many areas receive their business not because they actually continue to provide a competitive value, but because they are already a preapproved vendor. This inflexibility and lock-in, caused in part by the lack of effective systems for managing a large database of vendors, costs companies enormously, both financially and in reduced quality of products and services.

Research into this topic has actually made me consider whether a tool like Arena Solutions could be used primarily as a supplier management and collaboration tool. BOMs are complex objects; however, many other finished products and services that are much less complex would simply use a smaller proportion of Arena's overall functionality. Some may read this and respond that supplier management vendors already have this area covered. But a review of supplier management software did not leave me with the impression that this software market has been very well developed. In fact, this was once a red-hot software market (although artificially pumped up by the finance industry and stock market manipulations), led by the then well-known software vendors Commerce One and Ariba. However, since the dot com stock bubble burst, one does not hear very much about the supplier or vendor management software market (although paradoxically, there is a great deal of competition for the keywords of "supplier management" or "vendor management" for web search traffic). Supplier-relationship management or SRM is another term the software category is known by.

While supplier management/SRM software is neither a large nor vibrant software category, the need for this type of software is still very great. This area of functionality is not covered by ERP systems. ERP systems only contain the information necessary to enable transactions and execute preferential procurement agreements. In SAP ERP for instance, something called a quota arrangement allocates a company's demand to a specific supplier. But this is the second part of the process. ERP system functionality does not help you manage your supplier database in an analytical sense. Rather, the ERP system merely executes the policy that has been predetermined. Companies need software support to improve the management and intelligence of their supplier database and help make better supplier decisions.

CHAPTER 9

Reasons for Poor BOM
Management Design

This book focuses on software for the simple reason that the solutions for modern BOM management problems are primarily software-related. Up to this point, I have pointed out numerous examples where, what was once a major decision for many companies (e.g., whether to flatten the BOM or keep it hierarchical), is rendered irrelevant after an effective BOM Management System has been implemented, In this particular instance, the problem is solved because a BMMS can represent the BOM in multiple ways.

The number one reason for the poor design of current BOM management systems is that many companies don't have a comprehensive and fundamental understanding of the BOM and all of its associated data. As a result, they end up using dated approaches and software that is not up to the task of serving as the system of record for the BOM. Generally speaking, ERP vendors and consulting companies do not emphasize BOM management in a customized solution unless it is one of the weak PLM solutions offered by a major vendor. These PLM solutions are selected infrequently for implementation and when a PLM solution is selected, typically it is not relied upon to do much work. Because the BOM is implemented in so many applications (ERP, planning systems, etc.), the idea of a central BMMS is often not appreciated.

The Software Reasons for Poor BOM Management

The first enterprise system in which the BOM was encapsulated was the MRP system, followed by larger ERP systems that combined MRP and other supply and production planning procedures. ERP systems were designed to first meet the needs of finance and sales, and to a lesser degree manufacturing and supply chain. The major selling point of ERP systems was not that they provided particularly good functionality in any operational area. In actuality, they provided very basic functionality in these areas, but when anything occured in operations it was immediately reflected on the accounting side. When one compares the functionality depth in the SAP modules of Sales and Distribution (SD), Material Management (MM), Production Planning (PP) and Financial and Controlling modules (FI/CO), FI/CO is by far the deepest of them all.

ERP systems are transaction-processing systems concerned with making, moving and accounting for product. They are not designed to meet the needs of design or engineering. By the time computerized systems reached design, the ERP system had claimed ownership of the BOM. Integrating CAD/CAM with ERP systems essentially meant adopting the limited ERP view of the BOM, and boiling down the very rich set of BOM functionality and fields contained within the design and engineering system to fit this limited view. Secondly, as ERP systems are generally some of the largest and most expensive systems that any company buys, the ERP viewpoint has influenced senior decision makers into interpreting the BOM using the narrow view provided by the ERP system. If CAD/CAM systems had predated MRP and ERP systems, then the story would have been quite different. How far the supply chain and ERP functions have come in taking ownership of the BOM is reflected in the book, *Structuring the Bill of Material for MRP*, published 1971. At this time, Plossl and others focused on taking engineering BOMs and making them suitable for MRP systems. Interestingly, George Plossel had the following to say about the BOM. This quotation displays knowledge that is not often understood by supply chain professionals:

...we must remember that the bill of material is basically an engineering document. Historically, the function of the bill of material has been to define the product from the design point of view and from the design point of view only. But now, because we want to use the bill of material for purposes of material planning, we must re-define the product from the manufacturing and planning point of view.

The Consulting Company Reason for Poor BOM Management

The major consulting companies in information technology (IBM, Accenture, KPMG, Deloitte, Cap Gemini) make a lot of money from implementing ERP systems. They are unconcerned with BOM management efficiency. Instead, they are measured on billing hours, and the most billing hours are available for implementing the standard systems of the major monopoly vendors such as IBM, Oracle and SAP. As such, one could argue it simply is not in their financial interests to educate their clients on the shortcomings of the BOM solutions offered by the major ERP vendors. The consulting companies and the major ERP vendors are joined at the hip. The consulting companies attend major events like SAP's SAPPHIRE, and simply turn around and repeat the SAP message to their clients.

Even though there are several ways of making vast improvements to poor BOM management at a very reasonable cost, poor BOM management continues to be a problem at company after company. This problem has persisted since before there were really good BOM management solutions, and persists even now when these solutions exist. One cannot expect the major consulting companies to change this situation by bringing knowledge of good BOM management solutions to their clients.

The Executive Decision Makers and the Reasons for Poor BOM Management

Most senior executives consider that it's perfectly fine to manage the BOM in each system that uses it, rather than managing it in a centralized application. In my experience, most executives do not understand the strategic importance of the BOM and how difficult it is to manage properly without some type of specialized system. Secondly, many of the decision makers in the both the implementing companies and the consulting companies are not even aware that BOM management as is currently performed in companies is a problem, as they do not know any other way. In fact, some executives are so dedicated to reducing the number of interfaces that they can miss the importance of applications to improved efficiency. I have been told by several executives that efficiency is not a priority as they can hire more people if necessary (which by the way never seems to happen), and that the main focus of their IT project should be doing as much in one system as possible. Often the executive decision makers do not take into account the efficiency as well as quality improvements that come from a BMMS. A BMMS can do things that cannot be accomplished by simply hiring more people. In fact, the ability of the BMMS to improve the BOM management of the other systems is frequently misunderstood. Many executives only see the BMMS as another set of interfaces that must be written, without considering that the BMMS pays back the effort of interface development with far more efficient BOM management that improves all the applications that rely upon BOM information.

Conclusion

At the time of publication, this is the only book to focus on BOM management in software. BOM management is not a large software category in terms of sales, yet every company that manufactures or outsources manufacturing has to manage a bill of materials, and the vast majority of companies do so the hard way with antiquated approaches and software that is not designed for the task. Companies generally don't have an overarching strategy or vision for how to manage such a complicated master data object, or to distribute it properly within the enterprise and among the company's supply chain partners.

Low BOM management productivity is a major problem at the majority of companies that use BOMs. This chapter has described several reasons for this problem. One is that ERP systems set a low standard for BOM management, and this standard has since become accepted as how things are done. Most executives have never seen a demonstration of software like Arena Solutions, and furthermore, they are being told by the large vendors and consulting companies that the BOMs can be effectively managed in a disjointed fashion, or that they should focus on expensive and poorly-defined PLM solutions. These PLM solutions distract from the most important and needed functionality: to effectively manage a large number of BOMs. Furthermore, consulting companies, more concerned with their bottom line than the value of software provided to clients, have little financial incentive to recommend lower-cost BMMSs such as Arena Solutions, for which they do not have a group of experienced people on the bench ready to bill. Second, many consulting companies have not investigated Arena Solutions and, therefore, do not understand what it does. Third, recommending solutions that are not SAP, Oracle or IBM is always a problem for large consulting companies because they have partnerships with these companies and are expected to serve as a sales arm of the major software vendors. (This dynamic is a bit more complicated when it comes to IBM, which is both a consulting company and a software vendor, but one that sells their own products and has a very large and profitable SAP practice). However, the synopsis of this chapter is that poor BOM management practices are the most common practices in industry, and there are very few experts that truly "get" BOM management and the best software options that are available.

CHAPTER 10

Conclusion

The BOM is a straightforward list of relationships between a finished good and the products required to make the finished good. As described by Wikipedia:

> *A bill of materials implosion links component pieces to a major assembly, while a bill of materials "explosion" breaks apart each assembly or sub-assembly into its component parts.*

The most important steps to rectifying the problems with BOM management is to understand the BMMS and satellite application solution design, and to recognize that the BOM is complex enough and has sufficient collaborative requirements and archival needs to require its own specialized application. Once this concept is understood, the rest of BOM management can fall into place relatively quickly.

Putting the BOM in the Right Context

However, such a narrow view of the BOM is probably the first step in making an incorrect decision regarding a BOM management solution and approach. In fact, rather than starting off with a definition, the questions that should be asked are:

- What are all of your BOM requirements?

- How do your company's current systems meet these requirements?

In a BMMS, a BOM is associated with design files, supplier information, pricing and a host of other information that makes the BMMS software a powerful central hub of BOM information. All of this information allows the BOM to be used in innovative ways, many of which became in a sense automated. For instance, the simple multi-level BOM, when applied to the BMMS, allowed for changes to be made on subassemblies only, and for all the changes to percolate up to the overall BOM. Security can be placed on any subunit of the BOM— including down to the part—allowing suppliers and contract manufacturers to provide input on just that subunit while keeping the rest of the BOM hidden from their view. Also, the subunit in a sense becomes its own object and can be viewed across different BOMs, bringing out the similarities and connectedness between the BOMs that are often hidden from view, and allowing design to make decisions from a more informed and integrated viewpoint.

The BOM that is represented in the BMMS is made up of both the EBOM and the MBOM, but is not limited to the EBOM or MBOM. The BMMS can represent both types of BOMs seamlessly to design, engineering and to supply chain. Extracts can be created from the BMMS to support any system that relies upon BOM information.

What Following the Current Approach to BOM Management Means

The current approach to BOM management needs to be drastically rethought. It developed incrementally and was based upon leveraging a company's existing tools rather than designing tools specifically for BOM management. Spreadsheets could maintain BOM information, albeit in a limited way, and so people began to use them for that purpose. Because ERP systems had data areas that held BOM information, some companies began to maintain their BOM information partially in ERP systems, and then partially in other systems (again design and engineering do not work with ERP systems). These are both in effect "dead end" solutions for the problem of BOM management, and do not scale well and provide very limited BOM functionality. In effect, these "solutions" cost the company very little in the short term, yet imposed a heavy cost in terms of inefficiency, lost BOM information, lack of ability to collaborate with internal and external parties on BOM information, and a host of other issues. For instance, when a company does not have a BMMS, it must make unappealing decisions and spend time determining how it will configure the BOM to fit that decision (e.g., with a certain amount of nesting). However, with a BMMS, these decisions can be skipped; all the BOM detail is placed into the BMMS and then presented in ways that meet the requirements of any department. BOM data can be exported from the BMMS in the same flexible way.

Getting Rid of the Term PLM

I felt compelled to use the term PLM in the title of this book in order for people who use the term to find the book. PLM is not—and can never be—a single application, and there is no logic for continuing the use of the term PLM to describe any product. There is simply no logical defense for continuing use of this term. In general, the term is used to trick companies into buying the wrong solutions and focusing on the wrong things. Because companies are using the wrong terminology, the wrong concepts, and the wrong software, many of them that have invested years in PLM initiatives have extremely little to show for their efforts. If you follow the approaches laid out in this book, you won't have a uselelss PLM Server that no one uses.

The MBOM in Supply Chain Systems

This book focused on what happens to the BOM once it falls into the supply chain area. This miniature version of the BOM is shared among ERP and external planning systems. The BOM is an object upon which MRP was based, and MRP was later the basis for DRP. MRP takes the BOM and combines it with a routing, work centers, and lead times in order to know when to bring in material and when to schedule planned production orders to support the demand quantities and dates provided by demand planning. This approach was designed to show what happens to the BOM once it leaves design and engineering. By showing how the BOM appears in multiple supply chain systems, this book shows how limited the BOM is when compared to the BOM in a BMMS. One important first step to improving BOM management is to appreciate that the BOM, as understood in supply chain systems, is not the full representation of the BOM required by the company.

The Reactive Versus Strategic Approach to BOM Management

The development of the BMMS was really the first attempt to develop a strategic way of managing the BOM. Some BMMS vendors have thought through the process of managing the BOM at a very detailed level—at a far more detailed level, in fact, than their clients. Rather than managing the BOM by simply using whatever is already within the company, the BMMS manages the BOM based upon a company's actual requirements for BOM management. Those that seek to manage BOM information in a spreadsheet or ERP system should consider the real complexity associated with BOMs. As noted by Arena Solutions: "The modern product record often includes a complex set of hundreds to thousands of structured items."

What Drove the Development of the BMMS?

The design for BMMSs emerged from experiences with difficult problems. Erik Larkin described how the idea for Arena Solutions and the awareness of the opportunity for improved BOM management resulted from trying to manage the BOM for a very specialized type of product: Light and Motion, who in the 1990s, was making housing and lights for scuba divers to do underwater shooting. Manufacturers introduced new camera models every six months, and so the rate of change in the BOM was high. Unable to find a tool that would allow them to meet the requirements of this environment, Erik and his team decided to code their own.

The need for a collaborative BOM solution was further highlighted when the contract manufacturer with whom Light and Motion were collaborating on a new design could not access the same information as the design company. In fact, this background is one of the reasons that Arena Solutions was designed to be a SaaS application. As a consultant in BOM management for design and engineering, Erik learned that he could at least partially predict a company's likelihood of success with a new product introduction on the basis of how well it was able to manage its BOM information. And yet, in a time when we often hear about the high failure rate of new products, how often do we hear about the management of BOM information as a tool that can improve a company's odds? We hear about marketing prowess and the ability to gain shelf space, but we almost never hear about the technology that can improve the actual product. This is a testament to how much control marketing has over the perception of what areas of a company add value to a product. The general literature sees success or failure as depending primarily on marketing. What if this view is false? How much money are companies leaving on the table by emphasizing their marketing when those resources could be applied to investments that are more likely to improve the odds of new product success?

The Present BOM Design

The current BOM design is based upon a concept of disorganized and distributed BOM management that does not work very well and leaves large gaps in communication between departments and individuals both inside and outside of the company. The present repositories for the BOM, such as ERP and spreadsheets, were never designed to provide the appropriate level of functionality that is resident in the best BOM management applications. These flawed alternatives can be used as stopgaps, but can never be used to create a coherent combined repository of BOM information.

The current approach exists for a number of reasons. One major reason is a lack of appreciation for how the BOM is a highly-collaborative master data object that requires its own specialized repository and its own customized system for collaboration. Biased parties that lack BOM management design knowledge (such as the large consulting companies) reinforce the current BOM management design, and large software vendors are content to have their clients keep doing things in an inefficient and dated manner. To provide the broadest understanding of how the BOM is represented in a variety of applications, this book has presented the BOM as it is managed in spreadsheets, supply chain planning systems, ERP systems and the BMMS. However, the book proposes only one design for improved BOM management, and this design has the BMMS at the center, feeding BOM information to all of the other applications.

Collaboration

BMMS systems can be amazing environments for collaboration. They promote collaboration by automatically updating all information in a single location, meaning users now have a single source of BOM data that can be relied upon to be the most current. In addition, BMMSs allow for communication in ways similar to a social media website, with users only receiving notifications about those parts assigned to them. In all of the applications that I have reviewed at SCM Focus, I have never seen systems in the enterprise space as collaborative as a quality BMMS, and in fact the only comparative system is the social media websites. This is why a BMMS/PLM solution that is not SaaS-based is at a serious disadvantage against the BMMS applications that are SaaS-based.

A main emphasis of this book has been the power of Arena Solutions for collaboration. Those who bought the book without expecting this emphasis on collaboration may be surprised. However, collaboration is needed for BOM management.

Improved visibility and communication also benefit a company commercially. To begin with, the BMMS makes a company's BOM process more organized, which makes the company more desirable for suppliers to work with. Due to improved communication with suppliers, suppliers rework the product less, resulting in it costing less to work with the client company. Per part, the company simply uses less of the supplier's or contract manufacturer's resources. Secondly, the BMMS provides better cost information to the company than it had previously. It also has a comprehensive view of its volume, as the BMMS captures all parts that are identical, but which may be fractured across different parts that are not known to be associated. This means that the company provides the largest and most comprehensive part volumes to suppliers and contract manufacturers, which reduces price and improves the company's priority. Furthermore, the BMMS is a far superior bidding information system that gives the OEM a clearer picture of bidding changes and reduces its risk. This "intelligence" allows the OEM to quickly adjust when conditions and quotations change. Unless one has personally worked in costing and contract negotiation, it's difficult to communicate how powerful having this information can be. However, the benefits of providing more comprehensive volumes to supply chain partners should be obvious to anyone.

Therefore, the BMMS not only improves the internal operations of the company, but makes the company easier to work with, raising the company's profile and prominence with external parties. This is a positive win-win feedback loop if there ever was one. Most enterprise software only improves conditions in a few dimensions; BMMS improves conditions in multiple dimensions.

A BMMS can allow a high degree and wide range of collaboration only if it has a capable and nuanced authorization model. This book showed screenshots that demonstrate a highly- effective authorization system that not only controls permissions, but is designed to effectively manage security with a low level of effort.

Contracting Manufacturing, Suppliers and Outsourced Manufacturing

The increased tendency toward manufacturing outsourcing has been a major driver for increased cross-company collaboration on the BOM. Collaboration that was at one time performed within companies is now performed across companies. Companies have witnessed great increases in their collaboration needs, not only for BOM management but in multiple aspects of their business, yet software vendors have lagged by offering dated designs that restrict companies and their ability to perform cross-company collaboration. Areas such as production planning and scheduling also should be made more collaborative so that the OEMs and the contract manufacturers can share an application that controls the manufacture of a product for which the two companies share responsibility.

The Keys to Improved BOM Management

While most of the keys to improved BOM management are related to the use and selection of software, as of publication, this book is the only one that focuses on software. Many BOM management vendors come out of the design and engineering space, and don't necessarily translate very well to the supply chain world. For these reasons, it is difficult for executive decision makers to get the big picture as well as how to implement changes in specific applications. This book has attempted to clear the pathway to BOM management improvement by presenting the overall concept and specific applications.

As I stated in the introduction, most of the improvements recommended in this book are inexpensive, and BOM management improvement is mostly a function of adding a BMMS combined with improved knowledge of how to manage the BOM in the other applications that use it. In this book, I have proposed a simple and effective BOM management design that can be implemented at a low cost, and which should pay back its investment in a relatively short period of time. In this solution, the BMMS is the central repository of all BOM information. It feeds the other applications that use BOM data. This solution improves BOM management within each application, and creates an environment in which the company, suppliers and contract manufacturers can collaborate. The cost of such a solution is low, with Arena Solutions offering a per seat license that allows one to access all of the Arena functionality for roughly $80 per month. Companies concerned with this small outlay can start off with far fewer users. Of course, the application adds more value if more people can access it. However, I can add value to any client with a one-seat license of Arena, because while a one-seat license does not allow me to collaborate with anyone, I can still use it as the system of record for the BOM and as a BOM archival system.

It's an easy first decision is to purchase a BMMS. Not only is the per-seat cost of Arena low, but unlike the experience of purchasing most enterprise software, there is no negotiation with software salesmen and no lengthy software selection process. Anyone can sign up for a user account and begin using the Arena Solutions immediately. They can test the system for thirty days for free. Subsequently, they can sign up for just a few users to begin testing the system after the thirty-day trial expires. There is little risk as the offering is a SaaS solution, which can be cancelled at any time. Other application areas should be so lucky as to have the same terms.

BOM ROI

The ROI of a BMMS is more complicated to calculate than the ROI of most other enterprise applications. Many of the costs saving are soft and relate to long-term improvements that are difficult to quantify, such as how it improves the company's BOM database as an asset, leading to improved reusability. Secondly, a BMMS improves so many different systems that it can be challenging to trace each of the improvements. Systems that improve the operation of a narrow area of the business tend to be approved, but the ROI of a system that has so many distributed benefits can be overwhelming to approximate. However, the good news is that a BMMS can be cost justified if improvement in just one area can be measured.

Because Arena Solutions is simpler to implement than most other enterprise applications and requires less user training, its payback will generally be faster than the more difficult-to-implement systems that rely upon and are improved by the BMMS data. This is why it makes sense to place the BMMS implementation as early in the implementation schedule as possible. As a supply chain software implementation specialist, my job is easier if the BOM data is of better quality, and the likelihood for a successful supply chain software implementation is greater if the company already has a BMMS in place.

Author Profile

Shaun Snapp is the Managing Editor of SCM Focus. SCM Focus is one of the largest independent supply chain software analysis and educational sites on the Internet. After working at several of the largest consulting companies and at i2 Technologies, he became an independent consultant and later started SCM Focus. He maintains a strong interest in comparative software design, and works both in SAP APO, as well as with a variety of best-of-breed supply chain planning vendors. His ongoing relationships with these vendors keep him on the cutting edge of emerging technology.

Primary Sources of Information and Writing Topics

Shaun writes about topics with which he has first-hand experience. These topics range from recovering problematic implementations, to system configuration, to socializing complex software and supply chain concepts in the areas of demand planning, supply planning and production planning.

More broadly, he writes on topics supportive of these applications, which include master data parameter management, integration, analytics, simulation and bill of material management systems. He covers management aspects of enterprise software ranging from software policy to handling consulting partners on SAP projects. Shaun writes from an implementer's perspective and as a result, he focuses on how software is actually used in practice rather than its hypothetical use or "pure release note capabilities." Unlike many authors in enterprise software who keep their distance from discussing the realities of software implementation, he writes both on the problems as well as the successes of his software use, giving him a distinctive voice in the field.

Secondary Sources of Information
In addition to project experience, Shaun's interest in academic literature is a secondary source of information for his books and articles. Intrigued with the historical perspective of supply chain software, much of his writing is influenced by his readings and research into how different categories of supply chain software developed, evolved and finally became broadly used over time.

Covering the Latest Software Developments
Shaun is focused on supply chain software selections and implementation improvement through writing and consulting, bringing companies some of the newest technologies and methods. Some of the software developments that Shaun showcases at SCM Focus and in books at SCM Focus Press have yet to reach widespread adoption.

Education
Shaun has an undergraduate degree in business from the University of Hawaii, a Masters of Science in Maritime Management from the Maine Maritime Academy and a Masters of Science in Business Logistics from Penn State University. He has taught both logistics and SAP software.

Software Certifications
Shaun has been trained and/or certified in products from i2 Technologies, Servigistics, ToolsGroup and SAP (SD, DP, SNP, SPP, EWM).

Abbreviations

AML—Approved Manufacturers List

APS—Advanced Planning and Scheduling

AVL—Approved Vendor List

BOM—Bill of Material

BMMS—BOM Management System

CAD—Computer Aided Design

CAM—Computer Aided Manufacturing

CM—Contract Manufacturer

DC—Distribution Center

DRP—Distribution Requirements Planning

EMS—Electronic Manufacturing Service

ERP—Enterprise Resource Planning

JDM—Joint Design for Manufacture

MDM—Master Data Management

MPS—Master Production Schedule

MRP—Materials Requirements Planning

ODM—Original Design for Manufacture

OEM—Original Equipment Manufacturer

Links in the Book

Chapter 1

http://www.scmfocus.com/sapintegration/2011/11/15/
what-are-saps-vendor-integration-certifications-worth-on-projects/

http://www.scmfocus.com/writing-rules/

http://www.scmfocus.com/billofmaterials/

Chapter 2

http://www.scmfocus.com/supplychainmasterdata/2012/02/
an-approach-for-improving-master-data-maintenance-better-
than-mdm/

http://www.scmfocus.com/supplychainmasterdata/2011/04/
master-data-management-using-excel-and-powerpivot/

http://www.scmfocus.com/supplychainmasterdata/2010/06/
why-software-based-mdm-is-a-consulting-boondoggle/

http://www.scmfocus.com/supplychainmasterdata/2012/06/
master-data-management-in-the-cloud/

http://www.scmfocus.com/failedsupplychainconcepts/2010/10/eric-larkin-from-arena-solutions-on-companies-that-attempt-to-manage-their-boms-with-erp-software/

http://www.scmfocus.com/supplychainmasterdata/2012/06/master-data-management-in-the-cloud/

http://www.scmfocus.com/supplychainmasterdata/2011/04/master-data-management-using-excel-and-powerpivot/

Chapter 3

http://www.scmfocus.com/enterprisesoftwarepolicy/2012/06/10/sun-tzu-for-enterprise-software-vendors/

Chapter 4

http://www.scmfocus.com/demandplanning/2010/09/why-companies-are-selecting-the-wrong-supply-chain-demand-planning-systems/

Chapter 5

http://www.arenasolutions/partsaver

Chapter 6

http://www.scmfocus.com/sapplanning/2009/04/24/pds-vs-ppm-and-implications-for-bom-and-plm-management/

http://www.scmfocus.com/sapplanning/2009/04/24/pds-vs-ppm-and-implications-for-bom-and-plm-management/

http://www.scmfocus.com/sapplanning/2012/07/27/the-connection-between-boms-routings-work-centers-in-erp-and-ppms-pdss-in-apo/

http://www.scmfocus.com/sapplanning/2012/05/27/sub-contracting/

Chapter 7

http://www.scmfocus.com/demandplanning/2010/07/pivot-forecasting-renders-forecast-hierarchies-obsolete/

http://www.scmfocus.com/inventoryoptimizationmultiechelon/2011/04/sap-is-about-to-change-its-inventory-optimization-story/

http://www.scmfocus.com/servicepartsplanning/2009/04/21/is-sap-plm-for-real/

http://www.scmfocus.com/supplychainmasterdata/2010/09/why-demand-works-is-a-model-for-configutationdata-management/

http://www.scmfocus.com/sapplanning/trans-codes/

http://www.scmfocus.com/enterprisesoftwarepolicy/2012/06/10/sun-tzu-for-enterprise-software-vendors/

http://vimeo.com/16271846

Chapter 8

http://www.scmfocus.com/sapplanning/2009/05/09/ctm/

http://www.scmfocus.com/sapplanning/2012/07/24/synchronizing-integrated-factories-with-stock-transfers/

References and Associated Quotations

Beyond BOM 101: Next Generation Bills of Material Management. Arena Solutions, 2012. http://www.gleanster.com/open_docs/open_docs/beyond-bom-101-next-generation-bill-of-materials-management#.UFO4eo1lSrg.

Beyond Colored Folders and Spreadsheets: Next-Generation Document Control for the Medical Device Industry. Arena Solutions, 2012. http://www.arenasolutions.com/resources/articles/device-master-record.

Bill of Materials. Wikipedia. Last modified July 24, 2012. http://en.wikipedia.org/wiki/Bill_of_Materials.

Blind Men and an Elephant. Last modified August 26, 2012. http://en.wikipedia.org/wiki/Blind_men_and_an_elephant.

BOMs (PP-BD-BOM). SAP, 2001.

Clement, Jerry, Andy Coldrick, and John Sari. *Manufacturing Data Structures: Building Foundations for Excellence with Bills of Materials and Process Information.* Wiley, 1995.

Collaborative Tools for Product Development: A New Approach. Arena Solutions, 2011.

Contract Manufacturer. Last modified August 26, 2012. http://en.wikipedia.org/wiki/Contract_Manufacturer.

Dastmalchi, Bijan and Richard Vermeij. *Manufacturing Outsourcing: Seven Common Pitfalls to Avoid.* Arena Solutions, 2007.

Engineering Bill of Material: The Ins and Outs. Arena Solutions. http://www
.arenasolutions.com/resources/articles/engineering-bom.

5 Steps to Scaling Your Business When Your Competition Stumbles. Arena Solutions,
2011. http://www.arenasolutions.com/resources/articles/scaling-your-business.

Foxconn. Last modified September 6, 2012. http://en.wikipedia.org/wiki/Foxconn.

Garwood, Dave. *Bills of Material for a Lean Enterprise.* Dogwood Publishing
Company, 2010.

Hopp, Wallace J., and Mark L. Spearman. *Factory Physics: Foundations of
Manufacturing Management,* 2nd ed. McGraw-Hill Irwin, 2000.

How much of your production process should you outsource? Arena Solutions.
http://www.arenasolutions.com/resources/articles/how-much-of-your-
production-process-should-you-outsource.

Integrating SNP and PP/DS. SAP. http://help.sap.com/saphelp_scm40/helpdata/en/f1/
c2d837ffbf2424e10000009b38f889/content.htm.

Lehnert, Volker. *Authorizations in SAP Software: Design and Configuration.* SAP
Press, 2010.

Manufacturing Outsourcing: 7 Common Pitfalls to Avoid. Arena Solutions.
http://www.arenasolutions.com/resources/articles/manufacturing-outsourcing-
7-common-pitfalls-to-avoid.

*Manufacturing Outsourcing for Small and Mid-Size Companies: 10 Key Challenges &
How to Address Them.* Arena Solutions. http://www.arenasolutions.com/resources/
articles/manufacturing-outsourcing-challenges.

Master Data in Subcontracting. SAP. http://help.sap.com/saphelp_afs63/helpdata/en/
d8/d7bb048a1c11d4a6a10060086fd66b/content.htm.

PDM vs. PLM: A Data Perspective. Last modified July 23, 2010. http://beyondplm
.com/2010/07/23/pdm-vs-plm-a-data-perspective/.

PDM vs. PLM: It All Starts with PDM (Whitepaper). SolidWorks. http://www
.solidworks.co.il/Products/pdf/2009/WP_PDMWorks_SVE_FINAL.pdf.

PDX Viewer. Arena Solutions. http://www.arenasolutions.com/pdxviewer/.

Plossl, George and James A. Orlicky. *Structuring the Bill of Material for MRP.*
Routledge. (Author's note: The year of publication is unknown. Statements
regarding a 2003 publication date are for later editions. Orlicky was not performing
his consulting work in 2003, but back in the 1970s and 1980s. This is important
because it shows the nascent movement of engineering BOMs to MRP BOMs.)

Saaksvori, Antti and Anselmi Immonen. *Product LifeCycle Management,* 3rd ed. Springer, 2008.

SAP and Business by Design. http://plmtwine.com/2009/05/20/plm-prompt-sap-on-premise-vs-business-by-design/sap-business-by-design/.

Snapp, Shaun. *Supply Chain Forecasting Software.* SCM Focus Press, 2012.

System of Record. Last modified October 19, 2011. http://en.wikipedia.org/wiki/System_of_record.

Supply Chain Brutalization: Handbook for Contract Manufacturing, Walt Grischuk, Book Surge, 2009.

The Arena Solutions Guide to Outsourcing: Removing Barriers, Maintaining Boundaries (Whitepaper). Arena Solutions, 2011. http://www.whirlaway corporation.com/PDFs/KS-Outsourcing/Guidetooutsourcing.pdf.

Three Essential Tips for BOM Control. Arena Solutions, 2011.

3 Tips for Effective Product Revision Control and Communication. Arena Solutions, 2012. http://www10.mcadcafe.com/link/Arena-Solutions-3-Tips-Effective-Product-Revision-Control-Communication/36479/view.html.

Turning Great Designs Into Great Products: The Changing World of Mechanical Design. Arena Solutions, 2012. http://www.arenasolutions.com/static/resources/pdf/arena_wp_pdm.pdf.

Unix security. Last modified July 30, 2012. http://en.wikipedia.org/wiki/Unix_security.

Using Excel for Bill of Materials (BOM) Management. Arena Solutions. http://www.arenasolutions.com/resources/articles/excel-bill-of-materials.

Voskuil, Jos. *Where is My PLM Return on Investment?* Last modified June 15, 2009. http://virtualdutchman.com/2009/06/15/where-is-my-plm-return-on-investment-roi/.

Who Really Made Your Car? Restructuring and Geographic Change in the Auto Industry, Thomas H Klier and James Rubenstein, W E UpJohn Institute, 2008.

Index

www.ingramcontent.com/pod-product-compliance
Lightning Source LLC
Chambersburg PA
CBHW080526220326
41599CB00032B/6221